BUILDING A LEGAL PRACTICE ONE ARTICLE AT A TIME

DAVID ZETOONY

BUILDING A LEGAL PRACTICE ONE ARTICLE AT A TIME

Rainmaking
through
Publishing

Contents

Acknowledgments

Working among world-class lawyers provides a rare and unique laboratory when it comes to article writing. There is simply no shortage of thought leaders and best-in-class practitioners generating material with which to experiment. I would like to thank my colleagues who allowed me to tinker with, rewrite, or reengineer their articles as I was putting together this book; who graciously agreed to let me test different styles and theories on their content; and who allowed me to provide my thoughts and commentary on their already excellent work. Among others, these included Laurie Belony, Victoria Duxbury, Anthony George, Kevin Healy, Josh James, Philip Karmel, Danielle Mangogna, Becky Nelson, Steven Poplawski, and Jay Warren.

I'd also like to thank Jena Valdetero and Tamara Lakic for reviewing drafts of this book and providing valuable recommendations and insights, Steven Poplawski and Robert Klingler for recommending additional content, and Ramona Bailey for her editing assistance.

Finally and most importantly, I would like to thank Gretchen Fair, who has been a constant sounding board and an essential supporter of all of my projects, personal and professional.

About the Author

David A. Zetoony cochairs the United States data privacy and security practice at the international law firm of Greenberg Traurig LLP. Before joining Greenberg Traurig, he founded and then cochaired the global data privacy and security practice at the international law firm Bryan Cave Leighton Paisner LLP.

Mr. Zetoony graduated cum laude with a dual degree in history and policy studies from Rice University in Houston, Texas, and received his JD from the University of Virginia School of Law in Charlottesville, Virginia. He writes on issues of domestic and international data privacy and security law and has been repeatedly named as one of the top thought leaders in his field, receiving numerous JD Supra Readers' Choice awards and Lexology Thought Leadership awards. He was also identified by a prominent legal publisher as the most read outside counsel in any field from any law firm.

In addition to his practice, Mr. Zetoony often speaks to and teaches attorneys about how to successfully leverage article writing to help clients and generate business.

Foreword

Esra Krause, Senior Counsel,
Iovance Biotherapeutics, Inc.

As an in-house attorney, I am regularly asked by my client for clear and succinct advice. A corporate executive is not interested in the nuances of the law or its interpretations. All they want to know is: can we do this? Providing a lengthy treatise that requires time to digest and analyze is just as useful as providing them with an unmarked set of keys.

To supplement my knowledge of the law, I rely heavily on daily articles from outside counsel. In the privacy field, because laws keep changing often, I read everything that I can get my eyes on. With no shortage of work in a busy company, I don't have time to waste on rambling prose. What I need is advice that gets directly to the point on how to mitigate risk and increase revenue. A well-written article with a good title and actionable information immediately grabs my attention. In this book, David provides the tools to help outside counsel do exactly that: ensure that their writing connects with readers and respects one of their readers' most valuable commodities: time.

Three years ago, after weeks of reviewing and trying to decipher the General Data Protection Regulation (GDPR), I stumbled upon six free GDPR modules by David Zetoony. When I finished watching them, I immediately went to my CIO and told him we must hire this attorney. His work communicated not only his command of the subject but also his passion in advancing public knowledge in privacy. He laid out extremely complex topics in a clear, well-thought-out manner. Each module followed the same pattern, creating a repetitive familiarity that helped me to focus on the subject matter and not get distracted by changing structures or format. That is the type of writing that David teaches in this book: clear, short, focused, business-practical articles.

In law school, we were taught the *IRAC* method for case briefing: Issue, Rule, Analysis, and Conclusion. Condensing hundreds of pages into organized patterns, using a formulaic approach, was the only way to retain so much material. When developing his techniques for efficient writing, David takes a similar approach. He created a formula for every article, FAQ, and guide, which ultimately provides the reader structure and consistency. Not only is this straightforward approach a huge time saver, but it also immediately hooks the reader and makes them want to learn more.

This book also teaches outside counsel how to create long-lasting articles. A lot of the articles I get tend to be newscastings and are not necessarily shelf stable. David teaches you how to create articles that might be newsworthy but, more importantly, that someone will want to read and rely on for months to come.

I greatly appreciate a clear, consistent approach to writing. In fact, when I read articles by authors that do not follow a clear formula, I find myself frustrated and sometimes stop reading altogether to look for another source. In my mind, a succinct article conveys that the attorney is an expert in their field. Only an author who understands the law well can convey it with the minimum number of words. Once I find a writing style that I like, I sign up to follow the author, and before I know it, the attorney has created a relationship with me through their writing. And because I am already familiar with their work and enjoy their style, I tend to select them as my outside counsel.

For a profession that started off being paid by the word, it might be hard to break some old habits and realize that there is a more impactful way of writing. This book helps its readers do that. It lays out a clear path for outside counsel to reach their in-house counsel audience through smart, concise writing. David provides straightforward, practical advice and clever insights and outlines the pitfalls to avoid. Having worked with David,

I can tell you that he practices what he preaches. He doesn't use filler in his articles or his advice. He values in-house counsel's time and only writes what needs to be written. There are many knowledgeable attorneys, but this is what distinguishes attorneys like David and will keep me coming back.

Introduction

There are hundreds of paths up the mountain,
all leading in the same direction,
so it doesn't matter which path you take.
The only one wasting time is the one
who runs around and around the mountain,
telling everyone that his or her path is wrong.

—Hindu teaching

I started at an AmLaw 100 firm as a summer associate in 2002 and have spent the entirety of my career in "Big Law." As a first-year associate, I recall a constant emphasis on "relationship-based marketing." There were classes on how to do it; there were partners willing to mentor; there were even books, videos, retreats, posters, courses, and reminders . . . the list went on and on. Although every firm teaches relationship-based marketing slightly differently, the emphasis is always on building connections and relationships with friends, family, and colleagues and watching, over time, as some of those relationships grow into work. I remember asking one of the senior partners about article writing, and I remember distinctly what he told me: "Nobody has ever gotten a client from writing an article, but it's a good thing to do sometimes anyway."

It took me years to discover that was incorrect. People win, and retain, clients by writing articles; people also win, and retain, clients by speaking at conferences, giving webinars, and engaging in the host of activities that constitute "expertise-driven" marketing. Two decades later, having built a practice based on expertise-driven marketing, I try to mentor my own associates by taking a somewhat more Zen approach—there are many paths up the mountain of developing a practice.

That is not to say that all paths are equal. They certainly are not. Whether someone pursues a relationship-oriented marketing strategy or an expertise-oriented marketing strategy significantly impacts the tactics they should take to accomplish their marketing goals. It also can have a significant impact on the type of practice that they develop, the type of work that they pursue, and even the type of law that they choose.

For attorneys who are trying to develop a business development plan, a threshold question, therefore, might be "Should I focus on relationship building, or should I focus on expertise building?" While that sets up a false dichotomy as many successful attorneys utilize some aspects of relationship-driven marketing and some aspects of expertise-driven marketing, I think that it's a good and useful threshold question to ask. At the end of the day, time is the only commodity that we can't create more of, and, at some point, all of us must be purposeful about where we place the time that we dedicate to business development. That's a fancy way of saying that we can't do everything.

As a mid-level associate, I asked myself the question of whether I should focus on relationship building or expertise building. I remember my thought process in coming to an answer.

First, I reflected on the people and institutions that I hired in my personal life. When I was looking for a doctor, I wanted to find the "best" doctor. When I was looking for a contractor, I would read every review I could find and try to find the "best" contractor. When I was looking at colleges, I wanted to see the rankings for the "best" colleges. Although I had never worked as an in-house attorney, I knew that if I were a general counsel, I would look for the "best" person in the field and would likely select that person over friends and acquaintances. In essence, I wanted to become the type of attorney whom I would hire, and I would hire the attorney who could best demonstrate expertise.

Second, I was on a timetable. Associates were first considered for partner at my law firm in their eighth year, which meant that if I wanted to have the best chance of making partner, I had roughly five years to show my marketing potential. One of the core tenets I had learned about relationship marketing was that relationships are like "seeds," but you don't know if they are the type of seed that will grow into work in a year or the type that takes 20 years to sprout. I felt like I didn't have the luxury of waiting (and I certainly did not have the patience for it).

When those factors were combined, expertise-driven marketing simply made intuitive sense to me.

The decision to focus on expertise-driven marketing sent me down a largely trial-and-error path, and it took years for me to figure out what was, and was not, an effective way to convey expertise.

To give an example, when I was a senior associate I had the great idea that if I published an article in the journal of a top law school, people would know that I had expertise. I spent three months drafting an article, another three months placing it in the journal of a top-five law school, and another ten months waiting for it to be edited and then finally published. When it came out, I felt famous! I can guarantee that nobody reading this book read the article (or even heard of it). In fact, I'm quite sure that nobody in any company, corporation, or in-house legal department ever read it or heard about it. The closest that it came to the grace of human eyes was when I was at a conference and an associate director at the Federal Trade Commission came up to me and said that someone told him that he should put the article on his reading list. He pulled out a folded piece of paper from his wallet, unfolded it, and there it was—scribbled under dozens of other titles and book-hopefuls. Hundreds of hours invested that bought me a momentary sense of self-importance and a place at the bottom of the reading list of a government regulator who would never be my client. The whole endeavor could scarcely be called expertise-driven marketing.

In comparison, recently a popular legal news service that aggregates and tracks articles published by more than 900 law firms identified me as the most read outside counsel in the world.[1] I probably published more than 150 articles that year, which were read more than 200,000 times in various sources.

---

1. Statistic taken between September 2018 and September 2019 from Lexology.

Since then, I have been repeatedly ranked by Lexology as the No. 1 "content marketing thought leader" in my field and by JD Supra as the No. 1 most read data privacy attorney.

What changed between writing a journal article that had single-digit readership and becoming the most read outside counsel? I developed over time eight rules of article writing that shape and guide the topics I choose to write on, the style I choose to use, and even the places I choose to publish. This book explains those eight rules and teaches attorneys how to put them into practice.

One final note. The purpose of this book is not to compare the benefits of relationship-driven marketing and expertise-driven marketing. Rather, my hope is that this book helps short-circuit the learning experience for attorneys who have decided to start on the path of expertise-driven marketing, or for attorneys who have found themselves wandering on the path but who may not have a good sense of what they are doing right and what they are doing wrong.

How to Use This Book

Section I of this book discusses the principles and context of expertise-driven marketing. It talks about (and dispels) myths about article writing, discusses the core principles that drive expertise-driven marketing, and identifies similarities between relationship-driven marketing and expertise-driven marketing to help those who have focused on the former and who want to bridge a path to the latter.

Section II of this book contains my eight fundamental rules of effective article writing. Each rule is a distillation of a principle that, if followed, can help hone how you select article topics, tailor your writing style, and convey your expertise effectively. In each rule, I include examples of published articles that both illustrate and violate the rule. As my own practice focuses on data privacy and data security law, some of the examples are drawn from that area of practice, but because the rules are universal, I have included examples from specialties ranging from antitrust to labor and employment. In many cases, I take articles that were originally written by other attorneys and worked with those attorneys to modify their articles by applying the rules. With the original authors' permission, I republished their article and tracked readership in order to present empirical data concerning the effectiveness of the rules.

After each rule, I answer frequently asked questions that I have received about the rule and provide a quick-reference table with what practices to do and what practices to avoid. These quick reference sheets distill each rule into practice. They also function as a reminder of the salient points that underpin each rule for readers who may have read the book some time ago but come back to the chapter as a reference.

After each rule, I also include a worksheet. The worksheets are designed to help readers put each rule into practice. Many of the worksheets encourage readers to draft an article after each chapter. As a result, readers may, through the course of reading the book, produce ten or more articles of their own. The worksheets are designed to build off of each other and to be completed in a sequence.

Section III of this book contains some additional considerations that may help an author who is trying to build a reputation through article writing. Unlike Section II, which focuses on how to write, Section III discusses larger strategies about how to build a practice.

Several references and resources can be found in the appendices. Appendix A contains an exercise to help readers identify good titles and topics that are likely to be well received. Appendix B provides some easy-to-use examples of formulaic efficient writing structures (see Rule 1: Efficient Writing). Appendix C provides a template calendar for organizing and stockpiling articles (see Rule 7: Repetition and Stockpiling). Appendix D provides a one-page reminder of the drafting rules that can function as a quick checklist to evaluate your own articles.

SECTION I

Expertise-Driven Marketing

CHAPTER I

The Core Principle of Expertise-Driven Marketing

What exactly is expertise-driven marketing? Expertise-driven marketing is the concept of marketing yourself to existing and future clients based upon your expertise. It's that simple.

Of course, the million-dollar question is *how* to market your expertise. That goes to the core principle of expertise-driven marketing—you market expertise by being perceived as the "best" in your field.

How you do that is really driven by your target audience. For many outside counsel, the target audience is in-house attorneys (e.g., general counsel, deputy general counsel, assistant general counsel, etc.); that may not be universally true, however. Depending upon your specialty, the target audience might be nonlawyers (e.g., human resources directors), business contacts (e.g., chief financial officers), or others who help companies manage risk (e.g., chief compliance officers, risk managers, etc.).

Once you identify the audience that you are trying to target, ask yourself, "If I were an [in-house attorney, HR director, CFO, CCO, etc.] looking for the 'best' person in a particular field, where would I go?"

In my own practice area, in-house counsel are the primary target audience, and, putting myself in their shoes, I might go to the Internet and search for a topic to see who has written the most on it. Other in-house attorneys might listen to a speech or presentation to better understand the topic. In either scenario, an element of the selection process becomes the fact that in-house attorneys may be trying to elevate their own knowledge base through learning and may be seeking out those who they believe have the most knowledge on a topic to teach. With that context in mind, and with that particular audience, the most common way of demonstrating that you are the best in a legal field is to be the person to whom the in-house counsel turns for information.

If your target audience differs from mine (or even if it's the same), it's possible that your answer to the above question may differ from my own. For example, if you are an employee benefits attorney and your primary target audience is human resources directors, you might determine that if you were a human resources director, you would look to someone whose publications you find on a respected trade association website, like the website operated by the Society for Human Resource Management (SHRM), or maybe it would be someone whom you see speak at a prestigious annual conference. In either case, at the end of the day, expertise-driven marketing is simply about identifying where your target audience looks when they are trying to find the person who is the best and then taking steps to make sure that they find your name when they look there.

With that context, it's important to note that this book (and expertise-driven marketing through publications in general) is not for everyone. If your target audience is likely to look at a publication as their strategy for finding the best person, then this book is right for you. If you know that your target audience would never look at a publication to find the best person, put this book down, ask yourself where they would look, and create a strategy centered around that audience and the places they go to find expertise.

CHAPTER 2

Myths of Expertise-Driven Marketing

Before starting down the path of expertise-driven marketing, it's important to address—and dispel—some common myths, as they can inadvertently send you in the wrong direction or discourage you from investing the time needed to build a practice based upon your expertise.

MYTH NO. I: NOBODY HAS EVER GOTTEN WORK FROM WRITING AN ARTICLE

Wrong; they have.

I've heard this myth throughout my professional career, and it's simply false. Work comes from expertise-driven marketing all the time and in several ways.

First, expertise-driven marketing through article writing is an easy way to remind existing clients about your practice. As discussed further in Chapter 11, in which I describe my Rule 7 of article writing (Repetition and Stockpiling), one of the core ways to develop new work is to be top of mind to clients by reminding them, as often as possible, about the areas in which your practice excels. It's not that clients forget who you are or don't appreciate your legal talents, it's simply that every client has thousands of competing demands for their attention. Given all of those demands, it's easy (and natural) to slip into the out-of-sight out-of-mind mentality, such that when they have a project that is in your area of expertise, they may not think of you. Worse, they may think of another attorney in your field whom they happened to talk to, run into, or read about the day before their need arose. There are various ways of staying top of mind. You can periodically check in with clients on the telephone, take clients to lunch, or catch up during social conversations. That said, sending articles to clients is a great way to stay constantly at the top of their inboxes. Unlike many other client touchpoints, which lack the ability to scale (after all, you can really only have one lunch a day without impacting your waistline), you can transmit an article to a large client base simultaneously. I can't tell you how many times a client has reached out to me and said, "David—I got your article yesterday and it reminded me that I should call you about. . . ."

Second, expertise-driven marketing through article writing is a good way to proactively suggest how you might be able to assist clients. Put differently, many attorneys tend to be reactive when it comes to marketing. They wait for their client to have a problem or matter that is within their realm of practice, and only after their client reaches out to them about the problem do they begin to market their practice (i.e., their ability to help). Articles, by their nature, have a dual purpose. While one purpose is to convey to clients that you are an expert in a certain area, the other purpose is to *educate* your clients about a legal issue, an unforeseen risk, or a strategy for dealing with a risk. The education element of the article often exposes a client to information that they may not have known or risks that they did not consider. In other words, article writing can be a great way of educating a client who doesn't know that they need your help about the fact that they do. Proactive, not reactive.

Finally, article writing can be a great tool to help others sell you. Your partners, associates, and colleagues all have clients. They know the quality of your work already, and when one of their clients has a legal issue within your area of expertise, they hopefully are already referring work to you. Article writing allows you to arm them with soft marketing materials that they can easily share with their clients that explain (or validate) their recommendation. Put yourself in the shoes of a colleague whose client has a matter that falls within your area of expertise. Without a body of expertise-driven marketing, such as articles or speeches, the "pitch" by your colleague to sell your services sounds something like "I have a partner who knows how to do that." At base, that selling proposition is only marginally better than the cliché of "I know a guy who knows a guy who can help you out." With a body of articles, the pitch takes an entirely different tone and sounds something like "My partner is the preeminent thought leader on that issue. I've attached a couple of articles that he's published on just this topic." The message moves from "I know a guy" to "I know *the* guy."

If you still doubt the contribution of expertise-driven marketing to getting new work, consider a recent survey that found that 48 percent (i.e., half!) of business-to-business executives who are responsible for making purchase decisions said that reading thought leadership influenced their purchasing decision.[1] Indeed, 41 percent of decision makers said thought leadership not only led them to select a particular company or firm but also increased their willingness to pay a premium for the work.[2]

MYTH NO. 2: NOBODY EVER GETS A NEW CLIENT FROM WRITING AN ARTICLE

They do.

As I mentioned in the introduction, this is one of the first myths that was told to me about article writing. It is simply wrong. Let me repeat for emphasis: New clients absolutely come through article writing. Indeed, the vast majority of my clients have come through article writing.

Sometimes you can tell that a client comes to you as a direct result of an article that you have written because they tell you. Consider, for example, the following e-mail from an attorney at a $400 million annual revenue company:

---

1. *2020 B2B Thought Leadership Impact Study* 5, EDELMAN (Nov. 14, 2019), https://www.edelman.com/research/2020-b2b-thought-leadership-impact-study. The survey was conducted in 2019 among 1,164 U.S. business executives.
2. *Id.* at 12.

From: John Smith
To: Zetoony, David
Subject: Looking for privacy counsel

Hi David,

I am in-house counsel for ####, Inc. (operator of #####. com) and we are looking for outside counsel to assist us on an as-needed basis with the expert-level CCPA questions that are arising during our compliance preparations. Your articles on CCPA keep landing on my desk, so I thought I would reach out and see if you are available to discuss whether this would be a good fit.

Thanks.

John Smith

Associate General Counsel

#####, Inc.

Or the following voice message from a $1.2+ billion annual revenue company:

Voicemail Message

"Hey, David, this is #####, the Chief Compliance Officer of a company called ######## that's located in ########. We're a software company and I've seen your data privacy practical guide. I'd like to set up a call as we're in the process of looking to retain outside counsel and I just wondered if you had a couple minutes to talk. My number is ###-###-####. I'll send you an e-mail with my contact information as well, but I just wanted to say hello in person before doing that. Thank you."

Other times, the impact of an article is less direct and is combined with a relationship connection. For example, a number of years ago a partner of mine was visiting a contact of his who was general counsel of an airline. While he was waiting in the lobby of the general counsel's office, he noticed a book that I had authored on the coffee table. When the general counsel came out to meet him, my partner pointed to the book and said, "Did you know that guy is one of my partners?" The combination of the expertise-driven marketing (i.e., the book) and the relationship-driven marketing (the personal contact and the visit) led to a multiyear engagement covering a variety of interesting projects. As this example shows, oftentimes, expertise-driven marketing and relationship-driven marketing work hand in hand. Alone, neither would have been sufficient to bring in the project. While the client had my book on his coffee table for several months, he had not (and likely would not have without some form of prompting) picked up the telephone to call me. Similarly, while the client had a preexisting relationship with my partner, he had not (and likely would not have) considered displacing his current data privacy and security counsel just to send work my partner's way. It was the combination of the publication, which demonstrated expertise, and the relationship, which prompted access, that led to the engagement.

So where does the myth come from that you can't develop clients through article writing? I find that the myth is often perpetuated by attorneys who have tried to write articles but have not written them correctly and, therefore, have not had personal success using expertise-driven marketing. Unfortunately that describes a lot of attorneys. Decision makers routinely say that less than 20 percent of the articles that they read are "very good" or "excellent"; most are either "good," "mediocre," or "very poor."[3] Worse yet, 38 percent of decision makers report that after reading bad thought leadership, their respect or admiration for an organization actually decreases.[4] This book focuses on how to make sure that your articles fall into the "excellent" category that leads to new clients. It is worth pointing out that the double-edged nature of marketing (i.e., marketing done right leads to new clients; marketing done wrong loses clients) is not exclusive to expertise-driven marketing. The same principle applies to relationship-driven marketing. If you focus your energy on developing and maintaining relationships but do so in a way that insults, disrespects, or annoys potential clients, the

---

3. *Id.* at 13.
4. *Id.* at 15.

effort will lead to less work. The result would, of course, not be an indictment of relationship-driven marketing as a concept; it would reflect only one attorney's execution of the strategy.

MYTH NO. 3: YOU NEED A TITLE TO MARKET YOURSELF AS AN EXPERT

You don't.

When I started down the path of expertise-driven marketing, my initial thought was that there was no way to sell myself as having expertise unless formerly I had been a director or commissioner at a government agency and could use that title to convince clients of my expertise. Many younger attorneys may feel the same way about not having the word "partner" after their name.

Don't get me wrong, titles help. Indeed, leveraging a title can be its own form of expertise marketing. If a client has an issue dealing with a certain statute or a certain regulation, if you happen to be the person who drafted the statute or published the regulation, you can leverage that fact to demonstrate expertise.

That said, while titles may be proxies for expertise, they are not the only way of showing it. Article writing is a way to work around the fact that you lack a title that itself conveys expertise. Clients often will come to me with a specific problem or issue and ask for "*the* person" who is the expert in the field. Sometimes that person is a partner, sometimes they are counsel, and sometimes they are an associate. When I can respond to the request with something along the following lines, I have *never* had a client doubt or question the attorney's expertise or care what title followed their name:

> Jane,
>
> Thanks for the e-mail. I have attached several articles Megan has published on the topic and cc'd her in case you have any questions. As you'll see from the attachments, she is the preeminent thought leader in this field and has basically been cited by everyone wrestling with the topic.

If you can arm your colleagues with the ability to send that type of message, nobody will question the fact that your title is associate, counsel, or junior partner.

MYTH NO. 4: CLIENTS DON'T READ ARTICLES

They do.

In my experience, clients tend to read *more* articles than outside counsel. The reason is simple. Many in-house legal departments are resource constrained, and many in-house attorneys are responsible for several divergent areas of law. When a legal issue arises, they often look to short, practical articles to help them get their bearings in order to either solve their client's problem or get enough background to triage the issue and get the assistance of outside counsel.

You don't need to trust my anecdotal experience. A recent survey of business-to-business executives found that 53 percent of purchase decision makers spent at least an hour per week reading thought leadership.[5] Twenty percent of decision makers reported spending more than *four hours* each week reading thought leadership.[6]

MYTH NO. 5: WRITING A SINGLE ARTICLE IS EXPERTISE-DRIVEN MARKETING

It is not.

Writing *an* article is **not** expertise-driven marketing. Writing *many* articles **is** expertise-driven marketing.

Think of writing a single article like going to a single cocktail party that a client will be attending. Both might be good to do, but you would not characterize writing a single article as expertise-driven marketing any more than you would characterize going to one cocktail party as relationship-driven marketing. Expertise-driven marketing is focused on a long-term strategy of creating and conveying expertise and building a personal brand around that expertise. An expertise-driven marketing

---

5. *Id.* at 5.
6. *Id.* at 8.

strategy may begin with a single article, but it certainly does not end there.

MYTH NO. 6: WRITING THREE ARTICLES IS EXPERTISE-DRIVEN MARKETING

It is not.

During an evaluation, an associate whom I was supervising wrote that he had contributed greatly to expertise-driven marketing by writing three articles in the past year. While that is certainly a good start, expertise-driven marketing through article writing requires a significant investment of time and effort (see Rule 7: Repetition and Stockpiling) that goes well beyond a handful of articles. As I mentioned in the previous paragraph, equate article writing with a relationship-focused activity (e.g., having lunch with a client). Having three lunches in a year with various clients would be a good thing to do, but nobody would equate that (without more) with a concerted effort to engage in relationship-driven marketing. The same holds true for expertise-driven marketing through article writing. Writing three articles in a year is a good thing to do, but it should not be equated with a concerted effort to engage in expertise-driven marketing.

MYTH NO. 7: EXPERTS HAVE A "HALO" EFFECT

They do and they don't.

The idea of the halo effect is that if you build up a reputation for expertise that attracts clients, you can cross-sell other attorneys around you in different practice areas because clients will assume that because you have expertise, an attorney you refer must as well. In other words, they will assume that experts must practice with experts.

While there might be some merit to the halo effect, in my experience it has little (if any) direct impact on bringing in projects in other fields. To the contrary, clients who seek out attorneys who demonstrate themselves as experts through publications have a modus operandi—they seek out attorneys who demonstrate themselves as experts through publications. The net result is that when one of my clients has an issue outside of my area of expertise and asks for a recommendation, they typically are very receptive when I can refer them to an attorney who fits that MO. These attorneys, however, don't benefit from my "halo"—they have their own. Selling them is easy. They have created their own evidence of expertise through demonstrable publications. The same client is typically not receptive to attempts to refer attorneys who don't fit that MO.

So, for example, this type of e-mail tends to work:

John,

Thanks for the e-mail. I have attached several articles Megan has published on the topic and cc'd her in case you have any questions. As you'll see from the attachments, she is the preeminent expert in this field and has basically been cited by everyone wrestling with the topic.

This type of e-mail typically does not:

John,

Thanks for the e-mail. My partner is experienced with that topic. I would be happy to put you in touch with them to discuss.

That does not mean that experts don't have a positive overall impact on the brand of their organizations. They absolutely do. In a recent study, 88 percent of business-to-business purchasing decision makers reported that the thought leadership that they read from one member of an organization impacted their overall perception of that organization by increasing either their respect for the organization, their perception of the organization's capabilities, or their trust in the organization.[7]

So what does all this mean? Experts do create a halo from their thought leadership. While the halo enhances the overall brand of the organization to which they belong, which can indirectly mean that potential clients are more open to considering

---

7. *Id.* at 9.

the firm in the future, the halo does not in and of itself sell other practices or professionals.

MYTH NO. 8: WORK DRIVEN BY EXPERTISE-DRIVEN MARKETING IS NOT PORTABLE

Wrong. It is.

In many respects, work that comes from expertise-driven marketing may be more portable (i.e., will follow you if you change law firms) than other types of work.

If a client believes that you are the foremost expert in the field—i.e., the best—they are far more likely to follow you to a different firm if you were to go to one. Just as important, they are far more likely to stay at your firm if the person with whom they have the longest relationship were to leave. I can think of dozens of examples over the years where a "relationship" partner made a decision to lateral to a different firm and a client with whom they had a long-standing relationship moved all of their work to the new firm, *with the exception of* those projects and practice areas for which the client had retained us based upon our depth of expertise.

The reason is simple. If a client perceives a project as a commodity, then it does not matter who does the work as long as the work gets done. These types of matters will typically leave a firm if the relationship partner leaves or if the client has a new general counsel who has a stronger relationship at a different firm. In other words, if you are not the relationship partner and you decide to leave your firm, there is a low likelihood that the work would be portable. Conversely, if the relationship partner decides to leave your firm, there is a low likelihood that the work will stay with you.

If a client perceives a project as requiring expertise and you possess the best expertise, then it absolutely matters who does the work. In that case, nine times out of ten, if you leave your firm, the work will go with you (i.e., it's portable); if, instead, the relationship attorney leaves your firm, the work will stay with you (i.e., it's sticky). The net result is that unless a competing attorney can demonstrate that they have the same, or greater, expertise as you do, the matter is likely to stay with you regardless of where the client goes, where you go, or where a relationship partner goes.

MYTH NO. 9: YOU HAVE TO BE AN "EXPERT" TO ENGAGE IN EXPERTISE-DRIVEN MARKETING

You don't.

Expertise-driven marketing through article writing is a process. While sometimes you write on topics for which you are already a recognized "expert," other times you write because the article writing process helps you develop expertise as it forces you to learn, wrestle with, and explain a topic. Put differently, article writing and expertise are sometimes like the chicken and the egg—you can't really tell which came first, but you typically find them together.

MYTH NO. 10: PUBLISHING AN ARTICLE IS GIVING THE MILK AWAY FOR FREE

I've heard this concern off and on throughout my career. It sometimes goes like this:

> "If we publish the answer, why will clients need to come to us?"

or

> "Shouldn't we be charging clients for legal research? Why would we give it away for free?"

I have two responses to this.

The first is to think of yourself like the legal equivalent of Santa Claus in *Miracle on 34th Street*. If you are able to provide a client with something for free that they would need to pay someone else to provide, they are likely to remember the favor and come to you for their next project. Consider the following e-mail from a deputy general counsel at a $15 billion annual revenue company:

From: ###.####@#####.com
To: Zetoony, David
Subject: Thanks

David—

I recently found your Handbook of FAQs on Service Providers—CCPA. Thank you for putting together such a practical, informative and well-written document. The material has been extremely helpful to me and my team.

I'm sure you have asked yourself whether it is worthwhile to put together and publish these types of reference materials. Count me squarely in the heck-yeah-no-question category. I've forwarded the document to several of my colleagues already. There is a great deal of value in having such a straightforward reference document. I'll reach out to you if we need anything further but I want to make sure you know your team's hard work has not gone unnoticed.

Thanks again—######

Second, you build a practice not by taking on 0.25 hour engagements, but by taking on engagements of significant size. If, through a publication, I can answer a question that 40 of my clients may have and, by answering it, forfeit 0.25 billable hours that I might have billed 40 times via 40 teleconferences with 40 clients on the same topic, that is a "win." Sure, I could have billed ten billable hours (40 × 0.25), but the cost of those ten hours would be incredibly high (scheduling time, switching between clients, etc.). I would far rather identify two or three clients who need more significant help and focus on them, while at the same time making sure that my other 37 clients are getting the answers and information from me so that they don't feel like they have to turn to another attorney. In other words, article writing can be a win-win-win. It can ensure that your clients receive valuable information at a great value (i.e., free), it can help your clients spot for themselves whether they need more in-depth help via a larger project, and it can free up your time to focus on clients who need that in-depth help.

CHAPTER 3

Five Similarities between Expertise-Driven Marketing and Relationship-Driven Marketing

As discussed in the introduction, the purpose of this book is not to suggest that expertise-driven marketing is better than relationship-driven marketing. Either strategy, if applied correctly, can help an attorney become a rainmaker. Instead, the purpose of this book is to help attorneys who have embarked upon expertise-driven marketing to do so quickly and efficiently.

For those who are already very familiar with relationship-driven marketing, you may find more similarities between the two types of marketing strategies than you were expecting. The following are a few of the most prevalent similarities between rainmakers who use relationship-driven marketing and those who use expertise-driven marketing.

First, rainmakers who use relationship-driven strategies will tell you that it is hard work. They focus on business development every day and do so in a manner that is disciplined and efficient.

Rainmakers who use expertise-driven strategies will tell you the exact same thing. It is not easy to build and convey expertise, and, done correctly, it requires a daily investment of time. Unfortunately, there are no shortcuts. As is discussed throughout this book (see, e.g., Rule 7: Repetition and Stockpiling), building a practice through expertise-driven marketing, and specifically through article writing, is not about writing a single article or even ten articles. It's about repeatedly, systematically, and continuously conveying to your clients and potential clients your expertise.

Second, rainmakers who use relationship-driven strategies know that being a good lawyer is table stakes. No matter how strong your relationships are, people must have confidence in your legal skills.

This is even more true for rainmakers who use expertise-driven strategies. The core of expertise-driven marketing is to convey to clients and potential clients that you are the "best." In order to do so, it's simply not possible to be an "okay" attorney. You need to master your craft and continually focus on improving your practice.

Third, rainmakers who use relationship-driven strategies will tell you that luck is less important a factor than most people think. While luck plays some role in expertise-driven marketing, at the end of the day, the reason that we market is to minimize the amount of luck involved by maximizing the exposure and brand recognition that we have with clients.

For example, in the context of article writing, it's true that there is some element of luck involved when an in-house counsel who has a problem reads an article that you have written on the topic, as opposed to an article written by another attorney. On the other hand, if you have written two dozen articles about a topic, it's less "luck" that they find you and more "statistical inevitability."

Fourth, rainmakers who use relationship-driven strategies know to be narrow in terms of focus. You can't be everyone's best friend, nor should you try. It is far better to focus on a handful of people with whom you really have a deep trusted relationship than to attempt to be the go-to person for everyone you meet. Rainmakers who use expertise-driven strategies do the same. You simply can't be an expert in all fields, and, if you try, people will not believe that you have an expertise in anything.

Imagine walking into a doctor's office and complaining about an injured knee. You might believe the doctor when he says that he specializes in knees and not to worry because he is the best knee surgeon in town. If you then mentioned to him that your throat has also been bothering you, and he responds that throats are also his specialty, you might get a bit suspicious. Right around the time that you ask him for a recommendation for a dentist and he swaps his stethoscope for a tooth scaler, you would probably get out of your chair and leave.

It's the exact same thing when it comes to attorneys. Most attorneys know more than one area of law. Some have practiced in multiple areas for years and excel in multiple things. The knee-jerk reaction of many attorneys who embark upon expertise-driven marketing is to be the doctor in the analogy above and tout their expertise in one field, then another field, and yet another. That almost always backfires, and they end up undercutting the degree to which a client believes that they are an expert in any field with each field that they add on.

To provide a personal example, over the years, I have successfully defended companies against allegations that they violated the antitrust law, marketing and advertising laws, data security laws, and data privacy laws. When I first started writing articles, I jumped between topics. I would write one article on an antitrust topic. I might then write about the Federal Trade Commission's jurisdiction over certain advertising practices. I might jump next to an article about trends in data privacy or data security. It took me years to realize that no matter how good I thought I was in each of those topics, it is impossible to convey to clients that I have best-in-class expertise in antitrust, consumer protection, marketing, advertising, and data privacy and data security. I might as well put a stethoscope around my neck and a tooth scaler in my hand.

The truth, of course, is that while I may be *good* in each of these fields, I am not the *best* in all of them. I had to decide which of those fields I wanted to be the *best* in and then convey that expertise to clients. Years later, while I still find myself interested in recent advertising cases, you will rarely (if ever) find me writing an article about advertising law, unless it relates to data privacy.

Fifth, rainmakers who use relationship-driven marketing know that they have limited time, and, as a result, they need to leverage their time for the biggest impact. In other words, before investing in a new relationship, it's important to do a cost-benefit analysis. Activities that require a significant amount of time and have a low likelihood of success should be a low priority; activities that require a small amount of time and have a high likelihood of success should be a high priority.

Like relationship-driven marketers, expertise-driven marketers only have 24 hours in a day. As a result, it is useful to do a cost-benefit analysis every time you embark on a project. As will be discussed throughout this book, there are certain types of articles that require far greater investments of time. Rainmakers who utilize expertise-driven marketing learn over time to avoid those projects (see Rule 1: Efficient Writing, Rule 2: Short, and Rule 5: Recycling and the Rule of Threes). Similarly, there are certain types of articles that have a low likelihood of being read and a low likelihood of ultimately leading to new projects (see Rule 3: Business Practical and Rule 4: Shelf Stable). Avoid those projects as well. The key is to prioritize articles—and ways of writing—that require relatively small investments of time but that have a high likelihood of being read, a high likelihood of identifying you as an expert, and a high likelihood of attracting work. Deprioritize articles that require significant investments of time and are not likely to be read, inure to your brand, or attract new projects.

CHAPTER 4

Expertise-Driven Marketing Can Facilitate Relationships

I often refer to attorneys choosing between an expertise-driven marketing strategy and a relationship-driven marketing strategy. While I think that most attorneys do need to choose where to focus their marketing energy, it would be incorrect to assume that expertise-driven marketing cannot contribute to, create, or solidify a relationship. Similarly, it would be incorrect to assume that relationship-driven marketing cannot contribute to the creation of expertise.

Let me try to unpack that. Many of the deep meaningful professional relationships that I have formed center around expertise. They involve clients, friends, and colleagues whom I met as a result of an expertise-driven marketing activity—whether through article writing, speaking, or a shared interest in an academic topic. They are people who see the law in the same way that I do and who get excited by the same types of legal developments that I do. If this were high school, they would be in the same "geek" debate club or robotics team as me.

I am not the only one who believes that you can create relationships around ideas and expertise. Mike O'Horo, a legal business development motivator, published an interesting blog post on the topic. In it, he describes what he perceives to be the evolution of the business relationship. My recap probably will not do the concept justice, and I recommend reading the blog post itself.[1] That said, here were my takeaways.

In the legal community, the types of relationships that lead to business have changed between generations.

---

1. Mike O'Horo, *Relationships 3.0: The Idea Relationship Era*, ATTORNEY AT WORK (Apr. 24, 2018), https://www.attorneyatwork.com/relationships-3-0-the-idea-relationship-era/.

If you go back to the 1980s (when I was in elementary school), lawyers got business from clients with whom they had personal, close-proximity relationships. Clients were neighbors, golf buddies, country club members, or church friends. They were the people who served on the same boards or whose children went to the same schools. In essence, business relationships developed, often organically, from social friendships in a geographic community.

If you jump ahead to the 1990s, the structure of the business community started to change. As companies merged, consolidated, and became global, legal spend increasingly became managed out of an office that might be hundreds or thousands of miles away from the location in which a lawyer was needed. That meant that when an in-house counsel was looking for an attorney, they were far less likely to look to their local social network. While there were some "national" firms, those firms paled in size and geographic breadth compared to their equivalents today. As a result, even if an in-house attorney wanted to send work to the law firm of an attorney with whom they had a local social relationship, the odds were that the friend's law firm did not have on-the-ground resources across the country (or across the world). In that environment, the idea of developing a relationship to drive business morphed. Instead of investing time in developing social friendships that might lead to business, lawyers began investing time to understand their clients' professional lives. In other words, developing a relationship with a client meant trying to understand the client's business, their industry, their legal needs, and their company's strategic culture and values. That type of relationship building might focus more on weekly telephone calls, quarterly lunches, or organizing events for a client's legal department and less on local non-work-related social outings.

Moving into the 2000s, another evolution began to take hold within legal departments—particularly after the dot-com bubble burst in 2001 and the Great Recession in 2008. As revenues shrank, companies cut costs, which often meant raiding legal budgets. Declining legal budgets led many law departments to in-source commodity legal work. In-house counsel were viewed as "free" labor. If the salary of an in-house resource was a fixed sunk cost, better to have them draft another contract or handle another piece of litigation than to incur the marginal cost of retaining a law firm. The net result was that in-house attorneys had far more responsibilities and far less time. Going to lunch with outside counsel became a luxury, and attending a sponsored event, dinner, show, or activity with an outside counsel was viewed by some as a chore that detracted from scarce family time. What that generation of in-house counsel sought were resources that were efficient, added value, and could be identified when they wanted them (i.e., online) instead of through a series of in-person, get-to-know-you meetings. They also wanted (or needed) to do much of the work themselves and only retain outside counsel for issues that exceeded what they could reasonably be expected to know or master internally.

Mr. O'Horo's hypothesis (or, perhaps more aptly put, his thesis) is that in this generation, in-house counsel want to be able to learn most of what they need to know online and on their timetable. As they develop their own skills with available free resources (e.g., articles, webinars, and recordings), they are implicitly testing the knowledge base, reasoning, world view, and business approach of the attorneys who deliver the content. When they come across the same resource repeatedly and identify with a certain business-practical approach, tone, or style, they form a different kind of relationship—one that Mr. O'Horo describes as an "idea relationship." Over time, it is that relationship that he ascribes to the development of work.

In my own practice, I have seen the concept of idea relationships play out. I have had in-house counsel retain me and tell me that they have read dozens of my articles and, through them, "like the way that I think" about particular problems. The key, of course, to forming an idea relationship is making sure that the materials that you create demonstrate the way that you approach legal problems. Your articles must be more than merely reporting the news or summarizing a case; instead, they should show a client, or a potential client, the type of advice that they will receive if they retain you. (See Rule 3: Business Practical.)

SECTION II

Rules of Writing

CHAPTER 5

Rule 1: Efficient Writing

You don't have to reinvent the wheel, just attach it to a new wagon.

—Mark McCormack

Almost everyone suffers from the same initial challenge when writing an article—the blank page. There is no worse feeling than having a great article idea, setting aside time to begin drafting, and then staring at the dreaded blank computer screen.

The time that it takes to get into the article drafting mood or to find the right tone or voice is, from a business development standpoint, time that could be put to better uses. One of the first challenges, therefore, is how to cut down on wasted transition time so that any time you have to write is applied to writing articles themselves—not to surmounting the blank page.

Luckily, there is a relatively easy trick to avoid wasting time: formulaic, efficient writing.

Most lawyers already know what it means to write in a formulaic, efficient way. If you are a litigator, recall the first time that you drafted a motion. You probably took out the Federal Rules of Civil Procedure, started with a blank computer screen, and, through a painstaking process, pieced together the form and structure of your title page, table of contents, table of authorities, argument, and conclusion. Even within the argument section, it may have taken hours (or, in my case as a young associate, days) to navigate the right tone and structure for presenting an argument effectively. The second time you drafted a motion, of course, you did not start with a blank screen. Instead, you opened up your first motion and began modifying and changing the text to adapt it to a new case or a new issue. After writing a dozen motions, the process of building the argument and conveying it effectively became second nature. You used the same type of cover page, the same initial section on the procedural posture of the case, and the same recitation of the legal standard that the court should apply. Even within the argument section, you probably developed a cadence and preferred phrasing.

The process is similar for transactional attorneys. The first time a transactional attorney drafts an employment agreement or a licensing agreement takes time; after doing it a dozen times, it becomes second nature.

Regardless of the area of practice, attorneys gain efficiencies by developing a formulaic way of writing—something that can be replicated in structure and tone between projects and between clients. That is not to say, of course, that the substance between projects doesn't change. Of course it does. There are countless ways in which we deviate with each new project, and every contract or motion does not look the same. Starting with a formula does not necessarily lead you to the same result, but it does significantly speed up the process and lead to drafting efficiencies.

Although almost every attorney is used to formulaic writing when it comes to substantive legal work, very few apply formulaic writing to publications. One of the main reasons is that for many attorneys, article writing is not a habit. So, for example, if an attorney's practice focuses on licensing agreements, they may be drafting licensing agreements every day. With that level of frequency, it does not take long until putting together an agreement becomes as much second nature as tying shoes. That same attorney may decide to write an article once or twice a year. That level of infrequency means that the subconscious rote memory that they have for other types of writing is absent.

One solution to create a formulaic writing style is, of course, to force yourself into repetition. If instead of writing an article every couple of months you begin to write articles weekly or daily (see Rule 7: Repetition and Stockpiling), you will naturally develop formulaic, efficient article writing just as you have in other aspects of your practice.

Another solution, however, is to consciously develop a writing formula.

What do I mean by that?

When I started writing articles 15 years ago, each article differed not only in substance but also in tone and style. Some would be a page long, others would be ten pages long. Some would be written with section headings, others felt like editorials. In order to avoid the inefficiencies of transitioning between writing styles, one day I sat down and sketched out a format for a series of articles that I intended to write. Although the articles would be on completely different topics, each article would follow the exact same tone and format—down to the style of the title, the position of the paragraphs, and the length. The format that I chose looked something like this (italicized language to be consistent across articles):

**Title: *What In-House Counsel Need to Know about*
<<INSERT TOPIC>>**

<<INSERT PARAGRAPH DESCRIBING ISSUE>>

<<INSERT INTERESTING STATISTIC>>	<<INSERT INTERESTING STATISTIC>>	<<INSERT INTERESTING STATISTIC>>
<<INSERT INTERESTING STATISTIC>>	<<INSERT INTERESTING STATISTIC>>	<<INSERT INTERESTING STATISTIC>>

In-house counsel should consider the following when deciding upon a <<INSERT TOPIC>>

    <<INSERT CONSIDERATION 1>>
    <<INSERT CONSIDERATION 2>>
    <<INSERT CONSIDERATION 3>>
    <<INSERT CONSIDERATION 4>>
    <<INSERT CONSIDERATION 5>>

    ...

Once the formula was created, I applied it to a number of different topics. So, for example, the formula helped create the following article about corporate bring-your-own-device policies:

What In-House Counsel Need to Know About Bring Your Own Device ("BYOD") Policies

Many companies permit their employees to use personal mobile devices, such as smartphones and tablets, to access company-specific information, such as email, under a Bring Your Own Device ("BYOD") policy. BYOD policies can be popular for employees who want to use hand-picked devices and for employers who want to avoid the cost of providing and maintaining company-owned devices. Nonetheless, the use of company data on employee-owned devices implicates both security and privacy considerations.

23% Percentage of employees that are given corporate-issued smartphones.[1]	39% Percentage of companies that reported "security concerns" were the main inhibitor to full BYOD adoption.[2]	40% The percent of companies that offer BYOD to all employees.[3]
56 Minutes The amount of time per day that one study found employees waste using their mobile device for non-work activity.[4]		~60% Percent of employees that reported they use their mobile devices to access websites blocked by their company.[5]

1. Press Release, Gartner, Gartner Survey Shows That Mobile Device Adoption in the Workplace Is Not Yet Mature (Nov. 29, 2016), https://www.gartner.com/newsroom/id/3528217.
2. BYOD & Mobile Security: 2016 Spotlight Report 9, CROWD RESEARCH PARTNERS (2016), https://crowd researchpartners.com/wp-content/uploads/2017/07/BYOD-and-Mobile-Security-Report-2016.pdf.
3. Id. at 7.
4. How Much Time Are Your Employees Wasting on Their Phones?, BUS. NEWS DAILY, https://www.business newsdaily.com/10102-mobile-device-employee-distraction.html (last updated Mar. 17, 2020).
5. Id.

Consider the following when deciding upon a BYOD policy:

1. **Is the scope of your organization's control over employees' mobile devices consistent with the organization's interest?** Organizations should think about how much interest they have in knowing about their employees' mobile devices. The company's legitimate interest in information can be the basis from which a BYOD policy emerges. For example, if the organization simply wants to allow an employee to access work email on a mobile device, then the policies and restrictions should proceed with that focus.

2. **To what extent and for what purpose does the organization monitor employees' use of mobile devices?** Many servers create logs showing when an employee's device accessed the organization's server using certain authentication credentials. Such logs are often appropriate from a security perspective. To the extent that the organization wants to monitor more substantive actions by an employee on a mobile device, such monitoring should be in line with an appropriate purpose.

3. **What procedures are in place to restrict the transfer of data from the organization's network by way of the mobile device?** Organizations often protect against the risk that the organization's data will be "floating" on multiple devices by (a) limiting the types of data accessible to mobile devices (e.g., email) and (b) restricting, to the extent possible, how that data can be used on the mobile device (e.g., policies on copying and requiring certain security settings). Some organizations use sandboxed applications for accessing work-related email. Such apps open email in a program that is separate and apart from the native email system that is built into the device and they control aspects of the user's experience. For example, they may restrict the user from locally saving any emails, or attachments, to the user's device.

4. **For security purposes, does the organization require a minimum version of the operating system to be in place and fully patched before an employee can use a mobile device?** Minimum versions ensure that certain security protections and bug fixes are present on the device.

5. **Can data on a mobile device be remotely wiped? By whom?** A best practice for devices that contain confidential or sensitive organization information is to ensure that the data can be remotely deleted from the device by the organization if the device is stolen or the employee is terminated. This may be relatively easy for some organizations. For example, organizations that use sandboxed applications that permit employees to access email on the company's server—but do not store or cache data locally—can typically be deactivated relatively easily and in a manner that does not allow an unauthorized person who may possess the mobile device to gain any access to the company's

continued

system. To the extent that an employee was permitted to locally store work-related data (e.g., cache work emails locally, or download attachments), an employer should consider whether it has the right and the technical means to remotely wipe the entire device.

6. **What procedure is in place for an employee to report a missing mobile device?** Accidents happen to everyone, but their aftermath can determine whether they become catastrophes. Employees should have clear direction on how to report a missing device to the organization—perhaps through the IT department or help desk—so that the organization's device removal policy can be followed immediately.

7. **What steps does the organization take to socialize its mobile device policies?** Organizations often rely on their IT staff, self-help materials, and employee certifications to ensure (a) employee awareness of the organization policies and (b) enforcement of organization policies.

8. **Do the security measures in place match the sensitivity of the data accessed through the mobile device?** For employees that receive non-sensitive information, minimal restrictions may be appropriate. For employees that receive sensitive or confidential information, higher restrictions may be appropriate.

9. **Does the BYOD policy facilitate a wage and hour dispute?** Although BYOD programs are widely lauded for increased productivity and "off-the-clock" accessibility, this benefit can expose employers to potential wage-and-hour issues if the BYOD user is a nonexempt employee. If a nonexempt employee is permitted to use a mobile device for work related purposes after working hours, is there a policy that mandates that the employee must report the time that he worked? Is there an effective and efficient means for the employee to report such time?

10. **Does the BYOD policy expose the company to additional discovery costs?** In the event that the organization is involved in litigation or a government investigation, it could receive a request that the company review its electronic files for evidence that may be relevant to the case. In some situations, a BYOD policy may expose the employee's personal information—e.g., texts, images, emails, and files—to potential disclosure in the litigation. This is particularly true if, pursuant to the BYOD policy, the employee is instructed to use native communication systems on their personal device. For example, if the employee routinely texts clients or other employees from their mobile device. If the employee has not taken care to preserve relevant information—particularly after an investigation or a lawsuit is initiated—it could lead to allegations of evidence spoliation against the company.

The formula also created the following article on a completely different data privacy topic—monitoring employees in the workplace:

What In-House Counsel Need to Know About Monitoring Employees

Federal laws prohibit the interception of another's electronic communications, but these same laws have multiple exceptions that generally allow employers to monitor employees' email and internet use on employer-owned equipment or networks. As a result, under federal law, if a private-sector employee uses an organization's telephone or computer system, their employer is generally permitted to monitor their communications. That said, once the personal nature of a communication is determined, an employer's ability to continue monitoring the communication may be curtailed. For example, under the National Labor Relations Act, employers cannot electronically spy on certain types of concerted activity by employees about the terms and conditions of employment.

Although monitoring is broadly permitted under federal law, some states require that employers notify employees that they may be monitored. Even in states that do not require notice, employers often choose to provide notice since employees who think that they are being monitored are less likely to misuse corporate systems. It is good practice for an employer to have employees sign a consent or acknowledgment that monitoring may occur and to inform them that personal calls may not be made from particular telephones.

Employers may also monitor what an employee posts to social media. Some states prohibit employers from requesting that an employee provide his or her username and password to a social-media account in order for the employer to see content that was not published publicly. This would include, for example, posts that were made available only to an employee's friends or personal network. In addition, some states prohibit employers from requiring that their employees accept a friend request that would permit the employer to view friends-only social media posts. Finally, some states prohibit monitoring of telephone calls on an employer's telephone network without the consent of one or both parties to the communication.

~80%	2	15
Percent of employers who actively monitor their employees electronically.[1]	States that require private companies to provide notice to employees of electronic monitoring.[2]	States that introduced or considered legislation in 2016 prohibiting employers from requesting passwords to social media accounts.[3]

1. Romy Ribitzky, *Active Monitoring of Employees Rises to 78%*, ABC News, http://abcnews.go.com /Business/story?id=88319&page=1 (last updated Jan. 6, 2006).
2. These states are Connecticut (Conn. Gen. Stat. § 31-48d) and Delaware (Del. Code § 19-7-705). State Laws Related to Internet Privacy, Nat'l Conf. of State Legs., http://www.ncsl.org/research/tele communications-and-information-technology/state-laws-related-to-internet-privacy.aspx (last updated Jan. 27, 2020).
3. Access to Social Media Usernames and Passwords, Nat'l Conf. of State Legs., http://www.ncsl.org /research/telecommunications-and-information-technologyemployer-access-to-social-media-passwords -2013.aspx (last updated July 1, 2020).

What to consider when crafting an employee monitoring policy:

1. Does your organization publish an acceptable use policy?
2. If so, does the acceptable use policy explain what employees may and may not do over the Internet while at work?
3. Does the acceptable use policy explain the disciplinary consequences of violating the policy?
4. Do you have the ability to block or otherwise restrict access to Internet sites that are barred under the acceptable use policy?
5. Does your employee handbook make employees aware of monitoring?
6. Does the state in which the employee works require single or dual consent for monitoring telephone conversations, and have your employees consented?
7. If your organization monitors phone calls, do you have a policy to cease monitoring when a call is clearly personal in nature, and do you follow it?
8. Have you considered whether an employee might be able to argue that they have an expectation of privacy to their work emails or to their work phone calls?
9. Are you monitoring emails to or from password-protected personal accounts?
10. Are your employees using their own computer equipment to send emails or view the Internet?

. . . and the following article about using fingerprint identification technology:

What In-House Counsel Need to Know About Using Fingerprint Identification Technology

Fingerprint identification technology uses fingerprints to uniquely identify individuals. The technology has been used by law enforcement agencies for decades, and dozens of statutes regulate when government agencies may collect fingerprints, how they are permitted to use them, and with whom they can be shared.

Advances in fingerprint recognition software have led many private entities to begin using the technology to authenticate consumers. For example, many mobile devices have integrated fingerprint recognition technology to replace, or supplement, passwords or passcodes. Some employers are also using fingerprint recognition technology to increase the accuracy and efficiency of employee timekeeping systems.

There is currently no federal statute that expressly regulates private-sector use of fingerprint recognition software. Nonetheless, the FTC, which has authority to prevent unfair and deceptive practices, may proceed against companies that misrepresent how they use, secure, or disclose captured fingerprints or fingerprint geometry.

Numerous states have enacted statutes concerning the collection of fingerprints by government agencies, by accreditation boards, or in certain regulated industries (e.g., childcare and education). At least two states have also enacted statutes that govern the private sector's use of the technology outside of specific fields and applications. Those statutes generally require that if an organization "captures" a fingerprint's geometry, it must provide the consumer with notice and obtain their consent. In addition, if an organization stores fingerprint geometry, it must limit its disclosure to third parties, enact measures to secure the fingerprint from unauthorized access, and limit its retention after it is no longer needed. A number of additional states require that if a company collects fingerprints, it take steps to prevent the fingerprint from being acquired when in the process of being destroyed.

120 million Number of fingerprints held by one government agency.[1]	1 in 50,000 Probability of a false match claimed by one mobile device in conjunction with fingerprint recognition software.[2]
$5,000–$25,000 The range of possible fines and damages that could be assessed under state law for each violation of a fingerprint identification statute.[3]	
$1.5 million Largest class action settlement / judgment against a company for allegedly collecting fingerprints without providing proper notice and obtaining appropriate consent.[4]	

1. *Next Generation Identification (NGI) Monthly Fact Sheet*, Fed. Bureau of Investigation (Oct. 2017).
2. *About Touch ID Advanced Security Technology*, Apple (Sept. 11, 2017), https://support.apple.com/en-us/HT204587.
3. *See* 740 Ill. Comp. Stat. 14/20 (1)–(4); Tex. Bus. & Com. Code § 503.001(d).
4. Stipulation of Class Action Settlement, Sekura v. L.A. Tan Enters., Inc., Case No. 15-CH-16694 (Cir. Ct. Cook Cnty. Ill. June 20, 2016).

Consider the following when using fingerprint identification technology:

1. **Security.** Assess the risk that fingerprints and/or fingerprint geometry may be compromised and consider what steps can be reasonably taken to attempt to keep the information secure.
2. **Retention and Disposal.** Review your retention and disposal practices to see if they specify how long such information should be kept, and how it should be disposed of.
3. **Notice.** Consider providing clear notice to consumers or employees before capturing their fingerprints.
4. **Consent.** Consider obtaining opt-in consent before capturing or using fingerprints.
5. **Sharing**. Consider obtaining opt-in consent before sharing fingerprints or fingerprint geometry with any third parties.

In total, I leveraged the formula to create a series of 55 articles. On some level, drafting articles became somewhat like the old Mad Libs game I played as a child. Instead of inserting a "noun," "verb," "adjective," and "your favorite pet" to create a funny story, I would insert a description, a statistic, and a list of relevant considerations to create an article. That said, while the formula provided an outline and guidance and surmounted the "blank page" trap, it was not intended to be a hard-and-fast constraint. As can be seen by the three preceding examples, each article differed to some degree from the formula. Some articles had more background context, some had more statistics, and some had more considerations. From a time and efficiency perspective, however, by leveraging a formula, I was able to publish *ten times* the quantity of articles that would have been possible if I approached every article as a completely new writing project.

To be clear, the concept of formulaic efficient writing does not mean that you need to use the formula in the previous examples. Indeed, I am not even suggesting that you have to select one single format for all of your publications. There are countless ways to structure articles, and different structures are more conducive to different topics, audiences, or issues. The fundamental principle is less about the structure that you choose and more about the concept of choosing a structure.

As an example, several years after completing the aforementioned series, I created a new formula for a "frequently asked questions" series. The new structure was designed differently to address a different topic (i.e., all articles surrounded the same new statute) and a different audience (i.e., one more sophisticated that would already have a working knowledge of the statute). As I had done previously, before embarking upon the first article, I spent time sketching out—from a high level—a specific format that I thought would be conducive to each article in the series. The formula this time looked something like this:

Title: *Privacy FAQ:* <<INSERT QUESTION>>

The European Union's General Data Protection Regulation ("GDPR") is arguably the most comprehensive - and complex - data privacy regulation in the world. Although the GDPR went into force on May 25, 2018, there continues to be a great deal of confusion regarding the requirements of the GDPR.

To help address that confusion, we are publishing a multi-part series that discusses the questions most frequently asked by clients concerning the GDPR.

Question: <<INSERT QUESTION>>

Answer: <<INSERT SHORT ANSWER>>

<<INSERT EXPLANATION>>

I again leveraged the format on repeated articles—this time publishing more than 100 articles discussing different privacy or security topics.

While you should design your formula for expediency and ease, the main point of Rule 1 is that you should *never* start with a blank page, nor should you waste time trying to rediscover the right tone or style when drafting an article. If you choose a consistent tone, style, and structure, you can invest your time in the more worthwhile exercise of publishing substantively strong content.

There are numerous formulas that can satisfy Rule 1, but if you are looking for some tested frameworks to start experimenting with, some common—and effective—article formats have been included in Appendix B.

RULE 1: FREQUENTLY ASKED QUESTIONS

Question 1: Will Clients Recognize Your Formula?

Sometimes.

You have to remember that not all of your clients are reading all of your articles. Indeed, a client may only pick up one out of every ten articles that you write. The net result is that while you are aware that you are using a formula, a client who reads one of your articles every couple of months is not likely to pick up on the fact that your articles are written using a similar style, tone, and structure.

On the other hand, you will find that some clients are persistent readers of your articles and pick up nine out of ten articles that you write. Those clients are likely to identify that there is a similarity in tone and style among your articles.

Question 2: If a Client Recognizes Your Formula, Does That Look Bad?

Not at all.

We are all used to seeing consistent styles and structures in different publication sources and rarely, if ever, think that it "looks bad." If you need a real-life example, pick up two or three copies of the *New York Times* and compare articles written on different days in the same section (e.g., Science and Technology). While you may not have recognized it consciously, you will start to see similar styles, structures, and tones (i.e., formulas) develop. Far from detracting from the publication, the formulaic writing style helps you, as the reader, understand the content and know what to expect as you read through a new article. Indeed, I have had clients tell me that they started reading an article on some topic or other and halfway through the article say to themselves, "This sounds like something that David Zetoony would write," only to turn back to the top of the article and see my name. Being able to deliver recognizable content based upon a formula is a bonus, not a detractor, when it comes to branding.

Question 3: If You Don't Like Your Formula, Do You Have to Keep Using It?

No.

Formulas can, and do, evolve. If you don't enjoy your formula or find that it is making writing *less* efficient, you should not stick with it. It's important to remember, however, that just because a particular formula is not working does not mean that you should abandon the concept of formulaic efficient writing. Try modifying your formula until it feels "right" for the type of information that you are trying to convey and your writing style. Once you find a formula that works, also don't be afraid to continue to modify it as your writing develops. The point is not to lock yourself into a writing style that you hate, it's to help you find a formula that works well for you and speeds up the writing process.

Question 4: Does Your Formula Have to Work for Every Topic?

No.

Some topics may be more conducive to one type of formula; other topics may be more conducive to a different formula. If your formula does not work for a particular topic, you can consider either changing your topic to conform to the formula or developing a second formula that might be more conducive to a different line of inquiry. Either way, remember that Rule 1 is about efficient writing. Sometimes it is faster, easier, and more efficient to abandon a topic than to start from scratch. If you do start from scratch, don't treat the article as a one-off exception. Instead, think about how to develop a second formula that might itself be repurposed in other articles.

Question 5: Can You Borrow Someone Else's Article Structure?

Yes.

It's not a copyright violation and it is not unethical to borrow a writing style or a writing structure. One way to identify a formulaic efficient writing style is to read a number of successful and widely circulated articles written by other attorneys—even if those attorneys are in a completely different practice area. If you take one of those articles and deconstruct it, you may find a formula that can be used for other topics, and other areas of law.

Question 6: Is the Only Criterion When Designing a Formula That It Be Easy to Execute?

No.

Ideally the formula that you choose will help you meet the rest of the rules discussed in this book. So, for example, in Rule 2 we discuss the benefits of short articles. A formula that requires you to write two pages concerning a factual situation, three pages discussing historic interpretations of the law as applied to the situation, two pages concerning your views on the correct interpretation of the law, and two pages regarding how to apply your interpretation would not support Rule 2. Conversely, a formula that helps focus your writing about an issue into a page, or a couple of well-drafted paragraphs, would support and facilitate the application of Rule 2.

As you read through the different rules discussed in this book, consider coming back to your formula and revising it, as needed, to facilitate complying with each rule.

Rule 1: Reminders

Do	Don't Do
✓ Create an article structure that can be used and recycled.	✗ Start with a blank page each time you draft an article.
✓ Consider using a consistent introductory paragraph across articles or a series of articles.	✗ Write each article using a different tone.
✓ Consider using a consistent conclusory paragraph across articles, or a series of articles.	✗ Write each article using a different structure or format.
✓ Deviate, as needed, from any pre-built structure.	
✓ Reevaluate your article structure over time to ensure that it facilitates fast and efficient drafting.	
✓ Reevaluate your article structure over time to ensure that readers find it easy to understand.	

Rule 1: Worksheet

1. Brainstorm two article topics and write them down: Article 1: _____ Article 2: _____
2. Create an outline for Article 1, but while doing so think about making the structure "work" for both Article 1 and for Article 2. If you have difficulty creating an outline, look in Appendix B for examples.
3. Save three copies of the Article 1 outline.
4. Using the first copy of the outline, complete a draft of Article 1. Track the amount of time that it takes to complete a first draft of the article and write it down here: Article 1 Drafting Time: _____
5. Open the second copy of the outline, and use it to complete a draft of Article 2. Track the amount of time that it takes to complete a first draft of Article 2 and write it down here: Article 2 Drafting Time: _____
6. Consider any time savings achieved when drafting Article 2 (leveraging the outline and experience of drafting Article 1).
7. Open the third copy of the outline and consider what sections were easy and what sections were hard to replicate between both articles. Adjust the outline to remove sections that did not "work" between the two articles. Add any additional sections that you think would facilitate quickly drafting an article in the future.
8. Save the third copy of the outline and consider using it as the template for your next articles.

CHAPTER 6

Rule 2: Short

There's a great power in words, if you don't hitch too many of them together.

—Josh Billings

We all remember having to draft an essay in school. The first question on everyone's mind was the same—how many words does it need to be? Most teachers provided a word count or page limit: "Papers must be between ten and 20 pages, double spaced, 12 point font." The same thing always ran through my head— ten pages must mean a B and 20 pages must mean an A. After all, more words would demonstrate that you put in extra time and effort and really understood the material, right?

It took me years to understand that length is not a proxy for mastery. It took me several more years to understand that not only is length not required in order to demonstrate expertise, but it also has a negative impact when it comes to developing business.

Why?

First—and while this seems obvious to me now, it's something that took me years to understand and appreciate—writing longer articles takes more time. Take for example an article that I wrote for the Stanford Technology Law Review in 2011 titled "The 10 Year Anniversary of the FTC's Data Security Program: Has the Commission Finally Gotten Too Big for Its Breaches?"[1] The article is approximately 7,770 words or, double-spaced, about 30 pages. I can't recall how many hours it took to write, but needless to say—it was a lot. If I spent one hour per page, that would have been 30 hours (nearly a full work week). As

---

1. 2011 Stan. Tech. L. Rev. 12 (2011).

almost every writer knows, longer articles have increasing per-page time investments. You must expend time not just to put words on a page, but to edit, review, and revise all the pages collectively.

The net result is that one 30-page article can take more time than 30 one-page articles. In other words, the opportunity cost of the single long article is dozens of shorter articles. The question that I should have asked myself before beginning that project was "What would have a greater business development impact—one long article or 30 short articles?"

That question feeds into the second reason that long articles detract from business development—attention span.

There have been many articles over the past couple of years that quote statistics concerning the length (or lack thereof) of the human attention span. Perhaps one of the most cited is a study published by Microsoft that purportedly found that the average attention span fell from 12 seconds in the year 2000 to a measly eight seconds in more recent years. The "science" behind those statistics may be questionable, and, as a result, I won't quote any studies that suggest how long an article should be or how fast a potential reader should be able to read it.[2] On the other hand, there is a plethora of anecdotal evidence that most of us do not enjoy reading (and in fact do not read) long articles.

Think about your own reading habits. Put aside mandatory reading, i.e., having to read a 20-page case because you need to discuss it in a brief. Now think about the last three or four work-related articles that you read just because you were interested in the topic or a title caught your eye. How long were they? Were you able to finish them? Were any of them full-length journal articles? When was the last time that you remember sitting down and reading a full-length journal article?

Personally, I am not of the 144-character Twitter generation, but I also know that for my own reading habits, if I see an article that is about a page long on an interesting topic, I am likely to invest the two or three minutes to read through it. Conversely,

---

2. Simon Maybin, *Busting the Attention Span Myth*, BBC WORLD SERV. (Mar. 10, 2017), https://www.bbc.com/news/health-38896790.

I have a stack of papers 20 inches high in my office of articles that have interesting enough topics for me to print them out but that I never found the time to read because they were simply too long. They are in my "when I have time" pile. In reality, once a year when I clean out my office, I usually come upon my "when I have time" pile and push it into the recycle bin. As a result, I really should rename it the "when I have time, but I know that I never will" pile. I am not alone in preferring (and actually reading) shorter articles. When I ask clients what they like to read, the response is near universal—short articles that are to the point and are no more than a page (maybe two). In a recent survey of business-to-business procurement decision makers, 72 percent said that they consider "short and easy to absorb" articles to be the most compelling.[3]

The net result is that if you write a 30-page article, the chances are that it is not going to get read *and* you have forgone the opportunity to write 30 one-page articles, *each* of which would have had a far greater chance of being read. Collectively, the number of reads (and hence the amount of name recognition and exposure) that you would have garnered by writing 30 articles is simply exponentially greater than the number of reads that you garner by writing a single long article.

Of course, when it comes to length, you are not presented with a binary option—articles come in all shapes and sizes. For me, it was an evolution downward. I started writing law-review-type articles (e.g., 30–50 pages). I migrated toward shorter articles mostly for law-related magazines (e.g., six pages). I next moved on to writing for association newsletters (e.g., two pages). Finally, I moved to writing updates on discrete topics (e.g., one to two pages). Once I realized that my intended audience had very little time and short attention spans, I realized that writing less was more.

So how do you train yourself to write succinct and short articles? As discussed above, part of the equation is simply choosing

---

3. *2020 B2B Thought Leadership Impact Study 21*, Edelman (Nov. 14, 2019), https://www.edelman.com/research/2020-b2b-thought-leadership-impact-study.

publications that don't demand length. In other words, choose to write a self-published alert, or choose to write for a newsletter, instead of writing for a law review. The other part of the equation is avoiding unnecessary text in the articles that you do write. Take for example the following article:

Addressing Climate Change in Due Diligence for Real Estate Transactions

On November 23, 2018, the United States government released Volume II of its Fourth National Climate Assessment.[1] The report assesses the effects of the expected rise in sea levels resulting from global climate change, concluding that under one reasonably foreseeable scenario, it is likely that between $66 billion and $106 billion of real estate in the United States will be below sea level by 2050, with inundation from rising seas quadrupling that range of damage by 2100. Impacts of this magnitude make it likely that flood insurance will be significantly more costly—or not available at all in some areas—adversely affecting a property's marketability and mortgageability even before a flooding calamity occurs. When one considers that a 30-year mortgage issued in 2019 is scheduled for pay off in 2049, it is clear that the time has arrived to consider the effects of climate change when undertaking real estate due diligence.

In addition to identifying the potential for rising sea levels, the Fourth National Climate Assessment concludes that climate change may cause real estate assets to suffer damage from storm surge flooding, increases in the severity of storms, wildfires, saltwater intrusion into coastal aquifers, and elevated groundwater tables. Further damage will occur from the flooding of hazardous waste sites, erosion, and forest fires sparked under drought conditions. Hotter temperatures are also expected to make many areas of the United States far less habitable, adversely affecting real estate values. As explained below, each of these issues is an appropriate subject of real estate due diligence.

Moving Beyond the Traditional All Appropriate Inquiry

The All Appropriate Inquiries ("AAI") standard promulgated by the U.S. Environmental Protection Agency[2] has always been the beginning—rather than the end—of real estate due diligence, because the Phase I report that AAI requires does not address such potentially relevant issues as the presence of lead paint and asbestos-containing materials, contaminated drinking water, the presence of PCBs in underground or in-wall electric cables, radon, mold, poor indoor air quality, wetlands, whether the facility has the required permits to operate, or whether the facility is operating in compliance with environmental regulations and permit requirements. The AAI and most of these other issues look backward at potential legacy liabilities and the potential burden they would place on the future property owner. By contrast, the issue of climate change requires forward thinking to consider how the expected changes in future climate and related environmental conditions may affect the real estate asset.

Understanding the Meaning and Limitations of the FEMA Maps

A key aspect of real estate due diligence is scrutiny of the flood maps published by the Federal Emergency Management Agency ("FEMA"), but there is widespread confusion as to what these maps mean and how they are prepared. The maps identify areas within the 100-year and 500-year floodplains. FEMA describes the areas outside the 500-year floodplain as "areas of minimal flood hazard."[3] While that may have been correct in the past, it is no longer so.

The first step in using the FEMA maps is to understand the nomenclature. The so-called 100-year floodplain is the area that has a 1% annual chance of flooding. Over the course of a 30 year mortgage, there is a 26% likelihood of one or more floods in the 100-year flood plain.[4] The 500-year floodplain is the area that has a 0.2% annual chance of flooding. Over the course of a 30 year mortgage, there is a 6% likelihood of one or more floods in the 500-year floodplain.[5] These risks are substantial.

But the situation is more serious than one would infer from the FEMA maps. The maps themselves are predictions based on hydrologic models that utilize the limited available historical data. They are frequently wrong. For example, a neighborhood of Houston called Memorial City not within the FEMA-designated 500-year flood plain has experienced serious flooding three times in the last 10 years.[6] Errors in FEMA maps are hardly surprising, because predicting flooding requires analysis of the complex interaction of tides, storm surges, precipitation, the built environment, and other factors.

Federal law authorizes FEMA to take climate change and the resulting rise in sea levels and more serious storms into account in preparing flood plain maps,[7] but FEMA has failed to do so. Since climate change is expected to cause sea levels to rise by up to 8 feet (or even 11.5 feet in some areas) by 2100,[8] this deficiency is material.

If real estate is found to be in an area where flooding may be a significant risk, procuring flood insurance is a prudent expense, but it is no panacea. Most flood insurance available in the United States is made available under the National Flood Insurance Program operated by the federal government. Coverage limits for commercial properties are very low: $500,000 for damage to real property and $500,000 for damage to personal property. The program does not offer business interruption coverage. Additional property damage coverage and business interruption coverage are available from excess carriers, but the cost of premiums is likely to rise over time as insurance companies consider the additional flooding risks from rising seas and more intense storms. As a taste of what is to come, in 2017, Hurricane Harvey dumped 50 inches of rain on areas of Houston over a four-day period, causing massive flooding and $125 billion of damage to property.

Moreover, the National Flood Insurance Program is not being run on an actuarially sound basis. From 2005 to 2018, the program paid out $36 billion more than it charged in premiums, resulting in massive borrowing from the U.S. Treasury that the program has no hope of repaying.[9] In effect, the program is providing an enormous subsidy to property owners with real estate in areas susceptible to flood hazards. As recommended by a report

continued

issued by the U.S. Government Accountability Office,[10] it is foreseeable that at some point Congress will step in and require that flood insurance premiums be set at a level that is actuarially sound. This will cause premiums to skyrocket, resulting in an economic hit to real estate owners regardless of whether their properties experience flooding. Significant annual premium increases are occurring and are expected to continue to occur even under the law currently on the books.[11] Adding to the uncertainty, the National Flood Insurance Program has been operating on the basis of short-term reauthorization extensions; it will expire at 11:59 pm on December 21, 2018 unless reauthorized by Congress.[12]

In considering the effect of future flooding on a real estate asset, consideration should also be given to critical infrastructure that the asset relies on for potable water, the disposal of sanitary waste, and transportation.

Greenhouse Gas Regulations
Due diligence for climate change should also consider how a real estate asset will fare under current and future regulatory programs to reduce greenhouse gas emissions. The exact contours of these regulatory programs cannot be predicted with assurance, but what can be anticipated is that the price of electricity and fossil fuels is likely to increase substantially. Efforts may also be made to "shame" the owners of an inefficient building by requiring the posting of an "energy efficiency grade" by the front entrance, as will be required in New York City under Local Law 33 of 2018, enacted earlier this year.

In 2017, New York City Mayor De Blasio proposed a local law that would require costly energy retrofits of existing buildings whose energy efficiency falls short of the code requirements applicable to newly constructed buildings in the City.[13] As an indication of the costs the bill would impose, it has been opposed vigorously by trade associations representing the real estate industry.[14] The New York City Council is now considering a bill that would impose increasingly stringent limits on carbon emissions from non-rent regulated buildings with more than 25,000 square feet of floor area, with the goal of reducing those emissions by 80% by 2050.[15] Due diligence for a major real estate transaction should consider the energy efficiency of the real estate asset and the capital improvements that may be required under current and future laws.

New Building Code Provisions
Where coastal property is purchased for the purpose of development, care must be taken to determine whether building code requirements designed to address special flooding risks have been adopted (or are under consideration) in the relevant jurisdiction. Such requirements—which can significantly increase the costs of development—have been adopted by several coastal municipalities. For example, in New York City, the Department of Buildings requires new construction to take into account flooding at heights and in areas well beyond those identified in the effective FEMA maps.

Too Hot to Handle?

Finally, consideration should be given to whether the real estate asset is located in an area that might be rendered effectively uninhabitable by rising temperatures. In 40 years, Phoenix is expected to experience conditions above 100 degrees Fahrenheit four months a year, and more than five months a year by 2100.[16] By 2100, Phoenix may experience more than 100 days a year of temperatures above 110 degrees, and temperatures in Dallas are projected to be above 95 degrees for more than four months a year.[17] Real estate values can be expected to decline in such areas as populations and businesses move elsewhere.

Conclusion

Climate change is upon us, and its impact on real estate will be substantial. Prudence dictates climate-related due diligence when acquiring or financing real estate.

Notes

1. The report was prepared under the leadership of the National Oceanic and Atmospheric Administration by a team of 300 federal and nonfederal experts, pursuant to the Global Change Research Act of 1990. Prior to its release, the report was reviewed by 13 federal agencies and a committee of the National Academies of Sciences, Engineering, and Medicine.

2. 40 C.F.R. part 312.

3. *Flood Zones*, FED. EMERGENCY MGMT. AGENCY, https://www.fema.gov/flood-zones (last updated July 7, 2020).

4. $1.00 - 0.99^{30} = 0.26$.

5. $1.00 - 0.998^{30} = 0.06$.

6. Dara Lind, *The "500-Year" Flood, Explained: Why Houston Was So Underprepared for Hurricane Harvey*, VOX (Aug. 28, 2017), https://www.vox.com/science-and-health/2017/8/28/16211392/100-500 -year-flood-meaning.

7. 42 U.S.C. § 4101b(b)(3)(D).

8. FOURTH NAT'L CLIMATE ASSESSMENT (2018), *Chapter 8: Coastal Effects, available at* https://nca2018 .globalchange.gov/chapter/8/.

9. Ray Lehmann, *NFIP's $20.5B Debt to Taxpayers Could Grow after Florence*, INS. J. (Sept. 13, 2018), https://www.insurancejournal.com/blogs/right-street/2018/09/13/500996.htm.

10. *Flood Insurance: Comprehensive Reform Could Improve Solvency and Enhance Resilience*, U.S. GOV'T ACCOUNTABILITY OFF. (Apr. 2017), https://www.gao.gov/assets/690/684354.pdf.

11. 42 U.S.C. § 4015.

12. *Flood Insurance*, FED. EMERGENCY MGMT. AGENCY, https://www.fema.gov/national-flood-insurance -program/national-flood-insurance-program-reauthorization-guidance (last updated July 28, 2020).

13. *See* William Neuman, *De Blasio Vows to Cut Emissions in New York's Larger Buildings*, N.Y. TIMES (Sept. 14, 2017), *available at* https://www.nytimes.com/2017/09/14/nyregion/de-blasio-mayor-environ ment-buildings-emissions.html.

14. Danielle Muoio, *De Blasio's Energy Efficiency Mandates Languish with No Deal in Sight*, POLITICO (Apr. 25, 2018), https://www.politico.com/states/new-york/city-hall/story/2018/04/25/de-blasios-energy -efficiency-mandates-languish-with-no-deal-in-sight-382038.

15. NYC Council Int. 1253-2018, *available at* https://legistar.council.nyc.gov/LegislationDetail .aspx?ID=3761078&GUID=B938F26C-E9B9-4B9F-B981-1BB2BB52A486&Options=ID|Text|&Sea rch=1253-2018.

16. Heidi Cullen, *Think It's Hot Now? Just Wait*, N.Y. TIMES (Aug. 20, 2016), *available at* https://www .nytimes.com/interactive/2016/08/20/sunday-review/climate-change-hot-future.html?mcubz=0.

17. *Id.*

The article contains 1,709 words. Not all of the text, however, is essential to convey substantive information to the reader or to convey to the reader that the authors have expertise when it comes to environmental due diligence in real estate transactions. Removing superfluous language eliminates almost half of the text and brings the total word count to 970 words:

Addressing Climate Change in Due Diligence for Real Estate Transactions

~~On November 23, 2018, the United States government released Volume II of its Fourth National Climate Assessment.[†] The report assesses the effects of the expected rise in sea levels resulting from global climate change, concluding that under one reasonably foreseeable scenario, it is likely that between $66 billion and $106 billion of real estate in the United States will be below sea level by 2050, with inundation from rising seas quadrupling that range of damage by 2100. Impacts of this magnitude make it likely that flood insurance will be significantly more costly—or not available at all in some areas—adversely affecting a property's marketability and mortgageability even before a flooding calamity occurs. When one considers that a 30-year mortgage issued in 2019 is scheduled for pay off in 2049, it is clear that the time has arrived to consider the effects of climate change when undertaking real estate due diligence.~~ Climate change is expected to have a significant impact on existing real estate. According to a government assessment, by 2050 up to $106 billion of United States real estate will be below sea level. In addition to ~~identifying the potential for~~ rising sea levels, the ~~Fourth National Climate Assessment concludes~~ assessment concluded that climate change may cause real estate ~~assets to suffer~~ damage from storm surge flooding, ~~increases in the severity of storms,~~ wildfires, saltwater intrusion into coastal aquifers, ~~and~~ elevated groundwater tables. ~~Further damage will occur from the,~~ flooding of hazardous waste sites, erosion, and drought-induced forest fires ~~sparked under drought conditions. Hotter temperatures are also expected to make many areas of the United States far less habitable, adversely affecting real estate values. As explained below, each of these issues is an appropriate subject of real estate due diligence.~~

Comment: The purpose of the article is not to convince readers about the impact of climate change or even to convince readers that climate change will have a significant impact on real estate deals. Rather, the author is attempting to reach clients or potential clients who already accept that climate change may have an impact on a real estate transaction and may be looking to identify an attorney with expertise in evaluating that risk in due diligence. As a result, the introduction—including the statistics—can be eliminated without impacting the strength of the article.

Eliminating the statistics also (a) lowers the amount of research needed by the author to draft the article and (b) increases the shelf stability of the article by not anchoring it to a report from 2018. See Rule 4: Shelf Stable.

Comment: The list of negative impacts caused by climate change does not need to be exhaustive in order to explain the need for doing due diligence. A shorter list saves space and makes the article easier to digest.

While some of the most severe impacts of climate change may not materialize before 2050, real estate is a long term investment. Indeed it will be 2050 by the time that today's 30-year mortgages mature. Given the risks posed by climate change, investors should consider the following six things when conducting due diligence on a potential investment.

> Comment: See Rule 3: Business Practical.

~~Moving~~1. **Move** Beyond the Traditional All Appropriate Inquiry

The All Appropriate Inquiries ("AAI") standard promulgated by the U.S. Environmental Protection Agency[~~2~~1] has always been the beginning—rather than the end—of real estate due diligence~~, because the.~~ The AAI Phase I report ~~that AAI requires~~ does not address a multitude of known environmental risks such ~~potentially relevant issues as the presence of~~as lead paint ~~and,~~ asbestos~~-containing materials~~, contaminated drinking water, ~~the presence of~~ PCBs in underground or in-wall electric cables, radon, mold, and poor indoor air quality~~, wetlands, whether the facility has the required permits to operate, or whether the facility is operating in compliance with environmental regulations and permit requirements. The AAI and most of these other issues look.~~ The fundamental problem is that the AAI looks backward at ~~potential~~the burden legacy liabilities ~~and the potential burden they would~~ place on ~~the~~future property ~~owner. By contrast, the issue of climate change requires forward thinking to consider how the expected changes in future climate and related environmental conditions may affect the real estate asset~~owners. The AAI is not designed to address new risks that are expected to materialize from climate change.

> Comment: The list of deficiencies does not need to be exhaustive in order to explain the shortcomings of the standard.

~~Understanding~~2. **Understand** the ~~Meaning and~~ Limitations of ~~the~~ FEMA Maps

~~A key aspect of~~Traditional real estate due diligence ~~is~~involves scrutiny of ~~the~~flood maps published by the Federal Emergency Management Agency ("FEMA")~~, but there.~~ There is, however, widespread confusion as to what these maps mean and how they are prepared. ~~The~~ FEMA maps identify areas within the 100-year[2] and 500-year[3] floodplains~~. FEMA describes the areas;~~ areas outside the 500-year floodplain are referred to as "areas of minimal flood hazard."[~~3~~4] While that may have been correct in the past, it is no longer so.

~~The first step in using the FEMA maps is to understand the nomenclature. The so-called 100-year floodplain is the area that has a 1% annual chance of flooding. Over the course of a 30 year mortgage, there is a 26% likelihood of one or more floods in the 100-year flood plain.[4] The 500-year floodplain is the area that has a 0.2% annual chance of flooding. Over the course of a 30 year mortgage, there is a 6% likelihood of one or more floods in the 500-year floodplain.[5] These risks are substantial.~~

> Comment: The list of deficiencies does not need to be exhaustive in order to explain the shortcomings of the standard.

continued

~~But the situation is more serious than one would infer from the~~ FEMA maps. ~~The maps themselves~~ are predictions based on hydrologic models that utilize ~~the~~ limited ~~available~~ historical data. ~~They are frequently wrong. For example, a neighborhood of Houston called Memorial City not within the FEMA-designated 500-year flood plain has experienced serious flooding three times in the last 10 years.[6] Errors in FEMA maps are hardly surprising, because predicting flooding requires analysis of the complex interaction of tides, storm surges, precipitation, the built environment, and other factors.~~ As a result, they are frequently wrong. Moreover, when it comes to climate change, historic data are insufficient. Past performance really is—by definition—no guarantee of future expectations.

> Comment: The explanation regarding the nomenclature and meaning of FEMA maps is not essential to the business-practical information being conveyed in the article—i.e., how to conduct due diligence. While the information may convey the expertise of the author, it may be more effective in a footnote in order to decrease the overall size of the article and improve its readability.

~~Federal~~ While federal law authorizes FEMA to take climate change ~~and the resulting rise in sea levels and more serious storms~~ into account ~~in~~ when preparing ~~flood plain~~ maps,~~7~~5 but FEMA has failed to do so.~~8~~ ~~Since~~ Because climate change is expected to cause sea levels to rise by up to 8 feet (or even 11.5 feet in some areas) by 2100,~~9~~7 ~~this~~ that deficiency is material.

3. Don't Rely on Flood Insurance as the Sole Risk Mitigation

If real estate is found to be in an area where flooding may be a significant risk, ~~procuring~~ flood insurance ~~is a~~ may be prudent ~~expense~~, but it is no panacea. Most flood insurance ~~available~~ in the United States is made available under the National Flood Insurance Program operated by the federal government. Coverage limits for commercial properties are very low: $500,000 for damage to real property and $500,000 for damage to personal property. The program does not offer business interruption coverage. Additional property damage coverage and business interruption coverage ~~are~~ may be available from excess carriers, but ~~the cost of~~ premiums ~~is~~ are likely to rise over time ~~as insurance companies consider~~ with the additional flooding risks from rising seas and more intense storms. ~~As a taste of what is to come, in 2017, Hurricane Harvey dumped 50 inches of rain on areas of Houston over a four-day period, causing massive flooding and $125 billion of damage to property.~~

Moreover, the National Flood Insurance Program ~~is not being run on an actuarially sound basis~~ may not be sustainable. From 2005 to 2018, the program paid ~~out~~ $36 billion more than it charged in premiums, ~~resulting in massive borrowing from the U.S. Treasury that the program has no hope of repaying.~~~~10~~8 In effect, the program ~~is providing~~ provided an enormous subsidy to property owners with real estate in areas susceptible to flood hazards. ~~As recommended by a~~ That subsidy may stop. A report issued by the U.S. Government Accountability Office,~~11~~9 it is foreseeable recommended that ~~at some point~~ Congress ~~will step in and~~ require ~~that~~ flood insurance premiums to be set at ~~a level~~ levels that ~~is~~ are actuarially sound. ~~This will~~ That would cause premiums to skyrocket, ~~resulting in an economic hit to real estate owners~~

~~regardless of whether their properties experience~~
~~flooding. Significant annual premium increases are~~
~~occurring and are expected to continue to occur~~
~~even under the law currently on the books.[12] Adding~~
~~to the uncertainty, the National Flood Insurance~~
~~Program has been operating on the basis of short-~~
~~term reauthorization extensions; it will expire at 11:59~~
~~pm on December 21, 2018 unless reauthorized by~~
~~Congress.[13]~~ In considering the effect of future flooding on a real estate asset, consideration should also be given to critical infrastructure that the asset relies on for potable water, the disposal of sanitary waste, and transportation.

4. Greenhouse Gas Regulations and Increased Energy Costs
~~Due diligence for climate change should also consider how a real estate asset~~ ~~will fare under current and future~~ Cities across the country are considering regulatory programs to reduce greenhouse ~~gas emissions. The exact contours~~ ~~of these regulatory programs cannot be predicted with assurance, but what~~ ~~can be anticipated is that the price of electricity and fossil fuels is likely to~~ ~~increase substantially. Efforts may also be made to "shame" the owners of an~~ ~~inefficient building by requiring the posting of an "energy efficiency grade" by~~ ~~the front entrance, as will be required in~~ gases that could raise energy costs. For example, New York City ~~under Local Law 33 of 2018,~~ has enacted ~~earlier~~ ~~this year. In 2017, New York City Mayor De Blasio~~ ~~proposed~~ a local law ~~that would require~~ requiring costly energy retrofits of ~~existing~~ many buildings whose energy efficiency falls short of ~~the code requirements~~ ~~applicable to newly constructed buildings in the City.[14]~~ ~~As an indication of the costs the bill would impose,~~ ~~it has been opposed vigorously by trade associations~~ ~~representing the real estate industry.[15] The New York~~ ~~City Council is now considering a bill that would impose increasingly stringent~~ ~~limits on carbon emissions from non-rent regulated buildings with more than~~ ~~25,000 square feet of floor area, with the goal of reducing those emissions by~~ ~~80% by 2050.[16]~~ current code requirements.[10] Due diligence for a major real estate transaction should consider the energy efficiency of the real estate asset and the capital improvements that may be required under ~~current and~~ future laws.

5. New Building Code Provisions
Where coastal property is purchased for the purpose of development, care must be taken to determine whether building code requirements designed to address ~~special~~ flooding risks have been adopted (or are under consideration) ~~in the relevant jurisdiction.~~ Such requirements ~~—which can significantly~~ ~~increase the costs of development—~~ have been adopted by several coastal municipalities. For example, in New York City, the Department of Buildings

Comment: Additional explanation regarding the potential risk that the insurance program may not continue is arguably superfluous.

Comments:

Equivocation regarding the scope of future regulations is unnecessary.

Multiple examples of regulations in one jurisdiction are arguably superfluous.

continued

requires new construction to take into account flooding at heights and in areas well beyond those identified in the effective FEMA maps.

6. Too Hot to Handle?

Finally, ~~consideration should be given to whether~~climate change may impact the demand for real estate ~~asset is located in an area that might be rendered effectively uninhabitable by rising temperatures. In 40 years, Phoenix is expected to experience conditions above 100 degrees Fahrenheit four months a year, and more than five months a year by 2100.[17]~~in certain areas. By 2100, Phoenix may experience more than 100 days a year of temperatures above 110 degrees,[18] and temperatures in Dallas are projected to be above 95 degrees for more than four months a year.[19]12 Real estate values ~~can be expected to~~may decline in such areas ~~as~~if populations ~~and businesses~~ move elsewhere.

> Comment: Providing estimates for temperature variations in 40 years and then in 80 years is arguably superfluous.

~~Conclusion~~

~~Climate change is upon us, and its impact on real estate will be substantial. Prudence dictates climate-related due diligence when acquiring or financing real estate.~~

Notes

~~1. The report was prepared under the leadership of the National Oceanic and Atmospheric Administration by a team of 300 federal and nonfederal experts, pursuant to the Global Change Research Act of 1990. Prior to its release, the report was reviewed by 13 federal agencies and a committee of the National Academies of Sciences, Engineering, and Medicine.~~

2~~1~~. 40 C.F.R. part 312.

2. The "100-year floodplain" is the area that has a 1% annual chance of flooding. Given compounding year-over-year risk, over the course of a 30 year mortgage, there is a 26% likelihood of one or more floods $(1.00 - 0.99^{30} = 0.26)$.

3. The "500-year floodplain" is the area that has a 0.2% annual chance of flooding. Over the course of 30 years there is a 6% likelihood of one or more floods $(1.00 - 0.998^{30} = 0.06)$.

3~~4~~. *Flood Zones*, Fed. Emergency Mgmt. Agency, https://www.fema.gov/flood-zones (last updated July 7, 2020).

~~4. 1.00 − 0.99³⁰ = 0.26.~~

~~5. 1.00 − 0.998³⁰ = 0.06.~~

~~6. Dara Lind, The "500-Year" Flood, Explained: Why Houston Was So Underprepared for Hurricane Harvey, Vox (Aug. 28, 2017), https://www.vox.com/science-and-health/2017/8/28/16211392/100-500-year-flood-meaning.~~

7~~5~~. 42 U.S.C. § 4101b(b)(3)(D).

8~~6~~. Fourth Nat'l Climate Assessment (2018), *Chapter 8: Coastal Effects*, available at https://nca2018.globalchange.gov/chapter/8/.

9~~7~~. Ray Lehmann, *NFIP's $20.5B Debt to Taxpayers Could Grow after Florence*, Ins. J. (Sept. 13, 2018), https://www.insurancejournal.com/blogs/right-street/2018/09/13/500996.htm.

10~~8~~. *Flood Insurance: Comprehensive Reform Could Improve Solvency and Enhance Resilience*, U.S. Gov't Accountability Off. (Apr. 2017), https://www.gao.gov/assets/690/684354.pdf.

~~11. 42 U.S.C. § 4015.~~

~~12. Flood Insurance, Fed. Emergency Mgmt. Agency, https://www.fema.gov/national-flood-insurance-program/national-flood-insurance-program-reauthorization-guidance (last updated July 28, 2020).~~

~~13. See William Neuman, De Blasio Vows to Cut Emissions in New York's Larger Buildings, N.Y. Times (Sept. 14, 2017), available at https://www.nytimes.com/2017/09/14/nyregion/de-blasio-mayor-environment-buildings-emissions.html.~~

14. Danielle Muoio, ~~De Blasio's Energy Efficiency Mandates Languish with No Deal in Sight,~~ Politico ~~(Apr. 25, 2018),~~ https://www.politico.com/states/new-york/city-hall/story/2018/04/25/de-blasios-energy-efficiency-mandates-languish-with-no-deal-in-sight-382038

15. NYC Council Int. 1253-2018 , available at https://legistar.council.nyc.gov/LegislationDetail.aspx?ID=3761078&GUID=B938F26C-E9B9-4B9F-B981-1BB2BB52A486&Options=ID|Text|&Search=1253-2018.

9. See New York City Local Law 97, enacted on May 19, 2019, as part of the City's Climate Mobilization Act.

16. ~~Heidi Cullen, Think It's Hot Now? Just Wait, N.Y. Times (Aug. 20, 2016), available at https://www.nytimes.com/interactive/2016/08/20/sunday-review/climate-change-hot-future.html?mcubz=0.~~

~~17~~10. ~~Cullen, supra note 16.~~ Heidi Cullen, *Think It's Hot Now? Just Wait*, N.Y. Times (Aug. 20, 2016), *available at* https://www.nytimes.com/interactive/2016/08/20/sunday-review/climate-change-hot-future.html?mcubz=0.

Modified, and truncated, the final 970-word version of the article fits on three pages and appears to the reader as follows:

Addressing Climate Change in Due Diligence for Real Estate Transactions

Climate change is expected to have a significant impact on existing real estate. According to a government assessment, by 2050 up to $106 billion of United States real estate will be below sea level. In addition to rising sea levels, the assessment concluded that climate change may cause real estate damage from storm surge flooding, wildfires, saltwater intrusion into coastal aquifers, elevated groundwater tables, flooding of hazardous waste sites, erosion, and drought-induced forest fires.

While some of the most severe impacts of climate change may not materialize before 2050, real estate is a long term investment. Indeed it will be 2050 by the time that today's 30-year mortgages mature. Given the risks posed by climate change, investors should consider the following six things when conducting due diligence on a potential investment.

1. Move Beyond the Traditional All Appropriate Inquiry
The All Appropriate Inquiries ("AAI") standard promulgated by the U.S. Environmental Protection Agency[1] has always been the beginning—rather than the end—of real estate due diligence. The AAI Phase I report does not address a multitude of known environmental risks such as lead paint, asbestos, contaminated drinking water, PCBs in underground or in-wall electric cables, radon, mold, and poor indoor air quality. The fundamental problem is that the AAI looks backward at the burden legacy liabilities place on future property owners. The AAI is not designed to address new risks that are expected to materialize from climate change.

2. Understand the Limitations of FEMA Maps
Traditional real estate due diligence involves scrutiny of flood maps published by the Federal Emergency Management Agency ("FEMA"). There is, however, widespread confusion as to what these maps mean and how they are prepared.

continued

FEMA maps identify areas within the 100-year[2] and 500-year[3] floodplains; areas outside the 500-year floodplain are referred to as "areas of minimal flood hazard."[4] While that may have been correct in the past, it is no longer so.

FEMA maps are predictions based on hydrologic models that utilize limited historical data. As a result, they are frequently wrong. Moreover, when it comes to climate *change*, historic data are insufficient. Past performance really is—by definition—no guarantee of future expectations.

While federal law authorizes FEMA to take climate change into account when preparing maps,[5] FEMA has failed to do so. Because climate change is expected to cause sea levels to rise by up to 8 feet (or even 11.5 feet in some areas) by 2100,[6] that deficiency is material.

3. Don't Rely on Flood Insurance as the Sole Risk Mitigation

If real estate is found to be in an area where flooding may be a significant risk, flood insurance may be prudent, but it is no panacea. Most flood insurance in the United States is made available under the National Flood Insurance Program operated by the federal government. Coverage limits for commercial properties are very low: $500,000 for damage to real property and $500,000 for damage to personal property. The program does not offer business interruption coverage. Additional property damage coverage and business interruption coverage may be available from excess carriers, but premiums are likely to rise over time with the additional flooding risks from rising seas and more intense storms.

Moreover, the National Flood Insurance Program may not be sustainable. From 2005 to 2018, the program paid $36 billion more than it charged in premiums.[7] In effect, the program provided an enormous subsidy to property owners with real estate in areas susceptible to flood hazards. That subsidy may stop. A report issued by the U.S. Government Accountability Office[8] recommended that Congress require flood insurance premiums to be set at levels that are actuarially sound. That would cause premiums to skyrocket.

4. Greenhouse Gas Regulations and Increased Energy Costs

Cities across the country are considering regulatory programs to reduce greenhouse gases that could raise energy costs. For example, New York City has enacted a local law requiring costly energy retrofits of many buildings whose energy efficiency falls short of current code requirements.[9] Due diligence for a major real estate transaction should consider the energy efficiency of the real estate asset and the capital improvements that may be required under future laws.

5. New Building Code Provisions

Where coastal property is purchased for the purpose of development, care must be taken to determine whether building code requirements designed to address flooding risks have been adopted (or are under consideration). Such requirements have been adopted by several coastal municipalities. For example, in New York City, the Department of Buildings requires new construction to take into account flooding at heights and in areas well beyond those identified in the effective FEMA maps.

6. Too Hot to Handle?

Finally, climate change may impact the demand for real estate in certain areas. By 2100, Phoenix may experience more than 100 days a year of temperatures above 110 degrees, and temperatures in Dallas are projected to be above 95 degrees for more than four months a year.[10] Real estate values may decline in such areas if populations move elsewhere.

Notes

1 40 C.F.R. part 312.

2. The "100-year floodplain" is the area that has a 1% annual chance of flooding. Given compounding year-over-year risk, over the course of a 30 year mortgage, there is a 26% likelihood of one or more floods ($1.00 - 0.99^{30} = 0.26$).

3. The "500-year floodplain" is the area that has a 0.2% annual chance of flooding. Over the course of 30 years there is a 6% likelihood of one or more floods ($1.00 - 0.998^{30} = 0.06$).

4. *Flood Zones*, Fed. Emergency Mgmt. Agency, https://www.fema.gov/flood-zones (last updated July 7, 2020).

5. 42 U.S.C. § 4101b(b)(3)(D).

6. Fourth Nat'l Climate Assessment (2018), *Chapter 8: Coastal Effects, available at* https://nca2018.globalchange.gov/chapter/8/.

7. Ray Lehmann, *NFIP's $20.5B Debt to Taxpayers Could Grow after Florence*, Ins. J. (Sept. 13, 2018), https://www.insurancejournal.com/blogs/right-street/2018/09/13/500996.htm.

8. *Flood Insurance: Comprehensive Reform Could Improve Solvency and Enhance Resilience*, U.S. Gov't Accountability Off. (Apr. 2017), https://www.gao.gov/assets/690/684354.pdf.

9. See New York City Local Law 97, enacted on May 19, 2019, as part of the City's Climate Mobilization Act.

10. Heidi Cullen, *Think It's Hot Now? Just Wait*, N.Y. Times (Aug. 20, 2016), *available at* https://www.nytimes.com/interactive/2016/08/20/sunday-review/climate-change-hot-future.html?mcubz=0.

From a cost-of-authorship standpoint, shaving off 739 words (or nearly three double-spaced pages) would have saved the author significant time, which, from an opportunity-cost perspective, could mean drafting two articles instead of one (see Rule 7: Repetition and Stockpiling). From an effectiveness standpoint, the 43 percent reduction in size makes the article easier to read and, hence, more likely to be read. To test that theory, I asked the authors to republish the second version of the above article and then track the readership of version 1 and version 2 (see Rule 6: Metrics). The numbers prove the point; version 2 was read 2.3 times more than version 1.[4]

The combination of lower cost and greater reach means higher return on investment to the author.

---

4. Based upon Lexology metrics as of May 28, 2020.

Sometimes short article writing can be accomplished simply by asking yourself whether an article that you are working on, or have already published, can be subdivided into more manageable (and readable) smaller articles. Take for example the following article, which started out at 1,225 words:

Can a CCPA service provider refuse a deletion request from the business for whom it processes personal information or from the consumer itself?

Yes. Unless the CCPA service provider has contractually agreed otherwise, a service provider can refuse a deletion request from the business for whom it processes personal information for one of the reasons in CCPA § 1798.105(c), and has an implied right to refuse a deletion request from the consumer under CCPA § 1798.105(a).

The CCPA Right to Deletion

CCPA § 1798.105(a) allows a consumer to "request that a business delete any personal information about the consumer." A business may have service providers which process the requesting consumer's personal information on behalf of the business. When a consumer requests that a business delete personal information, the business must also "direct service providers" to delete the information as well under CCPA § 1798.105(c).

Refusing a Request From a Business

Although a business must "direct" service providers to delete data, CCPA § 1798.105(d) says that "a business *or a service provider* shall not be required to comply with a consumer's request to delete the consumer's information if it is necessary for the business *or a service provider* to maintain the consumer's information" (emphasis added) in order to do one of the following:

1. Complete the transaction for which the personal information was collected, provide a good or service requested by the consumer, or reasonably anticipated within the context of a business's ongoing business relationship with the consumer, or otherwise perform a contract between the business and the consumer.
2. Detect security incidents, protect against malicious, deceptive, fraudulent, or illegal activity; or prosecute those responsible for that activity.
3. Debug to identify and repair errors that impair existing intended functionality.
4. Exercise free speech, ensure the right of another consumer to exercise his or her right of free speech, or exercise another right provided for by law.

---

5. Comply with the California Electronic Communications Privacy Act pursuant to Chapter 3.6 (commencing with Section 1546) of Title 12 of Part 2 of the Penal Code.
6. Engage in public or peer-reviewed scientific, historical, or statistical research in the public interest that adheres to all other applicable ethics and privacy laws, when the businesses' deletion of the information is likely to render impossible or seriously impair the achievement of such research, if the consumer has provided informed consent.
7. To enable solely internal uses that are reasonably aligned with the expectations of the consumer based on the consumer's relationship with the business.
8. Comply with a legal obligation.
9. Otherwise use the consumer's personal information, internally, in a lawful manner that is compatible with the context in which the consumer provided the information.

If a service provider needs the personal information for one of the reasons listed above it may refuse the deletion request from the business.

Refusing a Request From a Consumer
In some scenarios, a consumer may incorrectly direct a deletion request directly to a service provider rather than to the business for which the service provider processes personal information. In this scenario a service provider can refuse the deletion request because CCPA § 1798.105(a) only allows service providers to request deletion from a *business*.

Additionally, a service provider deleting a consumer's personal information in response to a direct consumer request to the service provider could result in a loss of service provider status under the CCPA. Under CCPA § 1798.140(v), an entity is only a service provider if it is contractually prohibited from "retaining, using, or disclosing the personal information for any purpose other than for the specific purpose of performing the services specified in the contract for the business, or as otherwise permitted by [the CCPA]." Deleting consumer personal information absent the direction of a business could be considered a "use" of personal information for a purpose outside of performing the services for the business, and is arguably not permitted by the CCPA.

Although not currently required to do so, a service provider should consider directing a consumer making a request of them to the applicable business as the appropriate point of contact. The current draft of the CCPA's proposed regulations requires a service provider to direct a requestor to the applicable business.

Contractual Considerations
Although the CCPA does not itself require that a service provider honor a deletion request, a service provider may be contractually obligated to do so. Many businesses include a contractual provision in their agreement with a service provider requiring the service provider delete personal information

continued

that is processed on the business's behalf at the direction of the business. A less specific "reasonable assistance" provision is also common, which obligates the service provider to reasonably assist the business in fulfilling a deletion request. Although here a service provider retains an argument that facilitating deletion when not required to do so by the CCPA may not be "reasonable assistance," the existence of this provision signals that a business may be expecting the service provider to honor its deletion requests.

A business may assert that the contractual provisions of CCPA § 1798.140(v), which are required to meet the definition of "service provider," imply that a service provider must honor a business's deletion requests. However, CCPA § 1798.140(v) specifically allows a service provider to process personal information outside of its relationship to the service provider if such processing is "otherwise permitted by [the CCPA]." As discussed above, the CCPA permits a service provider to refuse a deletion request for the reasons in CCPA § 1798.105(d). This reading is supported by the fact that CCPA service provider agreements commonly contain a separate provision requiring a service provider honor a deletion request directed to it by the business (as discussed above). The regular inclusion of this provision shows that the requirements of CCPA § 1798.140(v) are not, by themselves, typically seen as requiring the service provider to honor deletion.

Beyond CCPA specific provisions, a business may argue that other provisions in the agreement with a service provider require deletion of personal information at a business's direction. If personal information fits the agreement's definition of confidential information, the confidentiality provision may require confidential information be deleted or returned at the disclosing party's direction. A provision where a service provider has agreed to abide by the business's privacy policy may also create an argument that the service provider must delete personal information, depending on the drafting of the provision and the privacy policy. If a data protection agreement containing the GDPR's required Article 28 processor provisions applies, the definition of "personal data" in those provisions may be broad enough to apply to CCPA personal information and thus require deletion. Rarely, an agreement may obligate a service provider to respond directly to deletion requests it receives from consumers. Both businesses and service providers should be aware of the complications of this type of arrangement, including verification issues.

Contractual Best Practices
Service providers should not contractually agree to honor all deletion requests if the service provider believes it may have a CCPA-permitted reason for refusal. On the other hand, a business should consider obligating a service provider to inform the business of its decision to refuse a deletion request, state which exception under CCPA § 1798.105(d) the service provider believes applies, and be liable for any damages incurred by the business arising out of the service provider's refusal.

While the preceding article satisfied Rule 1 in that it utilized a formulaic writing style (e.g., question, answer, and advice), its length made it a significant writing investment for a single article and inaccessible to readers with time limitations. With a minimum investment of additional time, the article can not only be shortened in overall word count but also subdivided into at least four independent stand-alone articles. For example, the original text can be divided into:

Article 1 (353 words)

Can a service provider refuse a deletion instruction from a business under the CCPA?

Yes. Unless a service provider has contractually agreed otherwise, they can refuse an instruction to delete information that they receive from their client (i.e., the business for whom the service provider was processing personal information).

The CCPA allows a consumer to "request that a business delete any personal information about the consumer."[1] When a consumer requests that a business delete personal information, the CCPA requires that a business "direct [its] service providers" to delete the information as well.[2]

Although a business must "direct" its service providers to delete data, the CCPA states that "a service provider shall not be required to comply with a consumer's request to delete the consumer's information if it is necessary for the business *or a service provider* to maintain the consumer's information" in order to accomplish one of nine exceptions. While some of those exceptions arguably apply only to the business's use of personal information, other exceptions may apply equally to the service provider's handling of data. These include:[3]

1. Detect security incidents, protect against malicious, deceptive, fraudulent, or illegal activity; or prosecute those responsible for that activity.
2. Debug to identify and repair errors that impair existing intended functionality.
3. Exercise free speech, ensure the right of another consumer to exercise his or her right of free speech, or exercise another right provided for by law.
4. Comply with the California Electronic Communications Privacy Act pursuant to Chapter 3.6 (commencing with Section 1546) of Title 12 of Part 2 of the Penal Code.

continued

> 5. To enable solely internal uses that are reasonably aligned with the expectations of the consumer based on the consumer's relationship with the business.
> 6. Comply with a legal obligation.
> 7. Otherwise use the consumer's personal information, internally, in a lawful manner that is compatible with the context in which the consumer provided the information.
>
> If a service provider needs the personal information for one of the reasons listed above it may refuse the deletion request from the business.
>
> **Notes**
> 1. CCPA § 1798.105(a).
> 2. CCPA § 1798.105(c).
> 3. CCPA § 1798.105(d) (emphasis added).
> 4. CCPA § 1798.105(a).

Article 2 (71 words)

> ### Can a service provider refuse a deletion request from a consumer under the CCPA?
>
> Yes.
>
> A consumer may incorrectly direct a deletion request to a service provider rather than to the business for which the service provider processes personal information. Service providers are permitted to refuse deletion requests that they receive directly from a consumer as the CCPA only allows consumers to request deletion from a *business*.[1]
>
> **Note**
> 1. CCPA § 1798.140(v).

Article 3 (260 words)

> ### Can a service provider process a deletion request that it receives from a consumer under the CCPA?
>
> Sometimes yes, and sometimes no.
>
> A consumer may incorrectly direct a deletion request to a service provider rather than to the business for which the service provider processes personal information.
>
> If a service provider receives such a deletion request and decides, on its own accord, whether to honor it, that action could result in the service provider losing its legal status as a "service provider" under the CCPA.

Specifically, the CCPA mandates that a service provider be contractually prohibited from "retaining, using, or disclosing the personal information for any purpose other than for the specific purpose of performing the services specified in the contract for the business, or as otherwise permitted by [the CCPA]." Deleting a consumer's personal information absent the direction of a business could be considered a "use" of personal information for a purpose outside of performing the services for the business. It should be noted that in some situations, however, a business may provide a service provider with specific instructions concerning how it should handle deletion requests that it receives. For example, some businesses may instruct their service providers to always honor and respond to such requests. In those situations, a service provider's destruction of the information at the behest of a business would be consistent with its contractual obligations.

Although not currently required to do so, the current draft of the CCPA's proposed regulations requires a service provider to direct a requestor to the applicable business.

Article 4 (462 words)

What type of contractual provisions are included within service provider agreements in connection with consumer deletion requests?

Although the CCPA does not itself require that a service provider honor a deletion request that it receives directly from a consumer, a service provider may be contractually obligated to do so.

Many businesses include a contractual provision in their agreement with a service provider requiring the service provider delete personal information that is processed on the business's behalf at the direction of the business. A less specific "reasonable assistance" provision is also common, which obligates the service provider to reasonably assist the business in fulfilling a deletion request. Although here a service provider retains an argument that facilitating deletion when not required to do so by the CCPA may not be "reasonable assistance," the existence of this provision signals that a business may be expecting the service provider to honor its deletion requests.

A business may assert that the contractual provisions of CCPA § 1798.140(v), which are required to meet the definition of "service provider," imply that a service provider must honor a business's deletion requests. However, CCPA § 1798.140(v) specifically allows a service provider to process personal information outside of its relationship to the service provider if such processing is "otherwise permitted by [the CCPA]." As discussed above, the CCPA permits a service provider to refuse a deletion request for the reasons in CCPA § 1798.105(d). This reading is supported by the fact that CCPA service provider agreements commonly contain a separate provision requiring a service provider honor a deletion request directed to it by the business (as discussed above). The regular inclusion of this provision shows that the requirements of CCPA § 1798.140(v) are not, by themselves, typically seen as requiring the service provider to honor deletion.

Beyond CCPA specific provisions, a business may argue that other provisions in the agreement with a service provider require deletion of personal information at a business's direction. If personal information fits the agreement's definition of confidential information, the confidentiality provision may require confidential information be deleted or returned at the disclosing party's direction. A provision where a service provider has agreed to abide by the business's privacy policy may also create an argument that the service provider must delete personal information, depending on the drafting of the provision and the privacy policy. If a data protection agreement containing the GDPR's required Article 28 processor provisions applies, the definition of "personal data" in those provisions may be broad enough to apply to CCPA personal information and thus require deletion. Rarely, an agreement may obligate a service provider to respond directly to deletion requests it receives from consumers. Both businesses and service providers should be aware of the complications of this type of arrangement, including verification issues.

The net effect is that for the same investment of time, the author could produce four publications that are individually more likely to be read than the original (as the reader can get through them in a short sitting) and collectively make the author at least four times more likely to be seen by a client or a potential client.

It's worth noting that the above example involved an element of rewriting. Put differently, the author originally drafted a long article, and the above examples illustrate how the author could have restructured and redrafted the individual paragraphs or subheadings within the article to form separate articles. The redrafting did not involve a substantial amount of time, but it did take effort. Had the author started off by wanting to write short articles, they could instead have utilized an efficient and formulaic writing style (Rule 1) that would have facilitated the short publications with virtually no rewriting (i.e., no additional effort). Consider, for example, the following article:

Technology v. the Law: The Future of E-Signatures in Real Estate

Summary

Technology is rapidly changing the way in which business is done. Consumers are growing used to an on demand service—whether that is in relation to their banking, shopping or leisure time. Arguably the B2B world, including within real estate, has been slower to react and embrace new ways of working. Could the developing technology and law around e-signatures be a game changer?

What is an e-signature?

The e-signature is not a new concept: the Electronic Communications Act 2000 and eIDAS permit the admissibility of an e-signature as evidence in legal proceedings.

There are many different ways of effecting an electronic signature onto a document: pasting a signature, typing a name, using a stylus on a touchscreen. The eIDAS Regulation (EU) No 910/2014 goes further in defining three types of electronic signature:

1. + A basic electronic signature which can be applied to a document, e.g. adding a scanned signature.
2. + An advanced electronic signature which is linked to the signatory, is capable of identifying the signatory and is created using signature creation data that the signer can use under their sole control.
3. + Finally, a qualified electronic signature which must meet advanced electronic signature requirements and be backed by a qualified certificate, issued by a trusted service provider.

What are the advantages of e-signatures?

Web-based signature platforms can be used for e-signing documents and offer a number of advantages over current practice. These include: ease of execution, reduced risk of errors in execution, enhanced security and ease of administration: they even tick the eco box (saving printing and posting). They are particularly useful where signatories are located abroad where historically a transaction could only move as fast as the courier carrying the documents.

So why haven't they been adopted more widely?

The problem that remains is the validity of electronic signatures - particularly around legislation that requires a document to be "signed" or executed as a deed.

The general approach of the courts has suggested that an electronic signature should satisfy a statutory requirement that something be signed. However, there have also been some curve balls including the decision in Cowthorpe Road 1-1A Freehold Limited v Wahedall where the court was adamant that only pen and paper would suffice.

The Law Commission attempted to provide some clarity on e-signatures in its 2018 consultation. It suggested that an electronic signature is capable of

continued

meeting legal requirements where there is an intention to authenticate the document, but sought views on whether legislative reform was necessary to improve confidence in the market and encourage a wider uptake of e-signatures in practice. We await the outcome of that consultation with interest.

Are e-signatures acceptable in real estate transactions?
In its 2016 practice note the Law Society acknowledged that the Land Registry and Land Charges Registry required wet-ink signatures on any paper versions of documents sent to them, and HMRC "would normally" expect to stamp a wet-ink version of the document with a wet-ink signature. Essentially this means that any real estate document that does not require registration at the Land Registry may be suitable for electronic signing and we are finding that our clients are increasingly keen to adopt this technology where possible.

Wholesale adoption of e-signatures across real estate may not, however, be too far off, in the light of the Land Registry's Digital Street initiative. In 2018 it trialled its "sign your mortgage deed" allowing borrowers to digitally sign their mortgage deed online and witnesses no longer needing to be present when the document is signed. This is a progressive move from HM Land Registry and shows its intention to move towards modernising and speeding up real estate transactions.

Could e-witnessing be next?
When executing a document as a deed using a sole signatory or swearing a statutory declaration, a witness is required. Might it be possible to witness electronic signatures by video conference or is physical presence always required? We have seen the use of video link to give evidence in court proceedings in a number of cases - could this pave the way for a wider acceptance of remote witnessing?

The Law Commission has suggested that it is "best practice" for the witness to be physically present and in the absence of clear statute or authority on the point the risks will be too great for most to take.

However, we welcome the Land Registry and Law Commission's interest in this subject and are confident that the Law Commission's consultation and its outcomes will encourage more use of e-signatures, paving the way for quicker, safer transactions in real estate and beyond in the years to come.

While the above article is 778 words, the author selected a writing formula that made each of the subsections capable of being independently excerpted and published. Specifically the section headings are designed as frequently asked questions and do not build on each other or rely upon each other for context. As a frequently asked question they could be published independently with a minimum of editing. The following shows how each of the subsections could become its own article. New words (i.e., not in the original) are underlined.

Article 1 (221 words)

FAQ E-Signatures in Real Estate: <u>What is an e-signature?</u>

Technology is rapidly changing the way in which business is done. Consumers are growing used to an on demand service—whether that is in relation to their banking, shopping or leisure time. Arguably the B2B world, including within real estate, has been slower to react and embrace new ways of working. <u>This FAQ series is designed to help the real estate industry better understand (and embrace) e-signatures.</u>

What is an e-signature?

The e-signature is not a new concept: the Electronic Communications Act 2000 and eIDAS permit the admissibility of an e-signature as evidence in legal proceedings.

There are many different ways of effecting an electronic signature onto a document: pasting a signature, typing a name, using a stylus on a touchscreen. The eIDAS Regulation (EU) No 910/2014 goes further in defining three types of electronic signature:

1. + A basic electronic signature which can be applied to a document, e.g. adding a scanned signature.
2. + An advanced electronic signature which is linked to the signatory, is capable of identifying the signatory and is created using signature creation data that the signer can use under their sole control.
3. + Finally, a qualified electronic signature which must meet advanced electronic signature requirements and be backed by a qualified certificate, issued by a trusted service provider.

Article 2 (153 words)

FAQ E-Signatures in Real Estate: <u>What are the advantages of e-signatures?</u>

Technology is rapidly changing the way in which business is done. Consumers are growing used to an on demand service—whether that is in relation to their banking, shopping or leisure time. Arguably the B2B world, including within real estate, has been slower to react and embrace new ways of working. <u>This FAQ series is designed to help the real estate industry better understand (and embrace) e-signatures.</u>

What are the advantages of e-signatures?

Web-based signature platforms can be used for e-signing documents and offer a number of advantages over current practice. These include: ease of execution, reduced risk of errors in execution, enhanced security and ease of administration: they even tick the eco box (saving printing and posting). They are particularly useful where signatories are located abroad where historically a transaction could only move as fast as the courier carrying the documents.

Article 3 (232 words)

FAQ E-Signatures in Real Estate: <u>Why haven't e-signatures been adopted more widely?</u>

Technology is rapidly changing the way in which business is done. Consumers are growing used to an on demand service—whether that is in relation to their banking, shopping or leisure time. Arguably the B2B world, including within real estate, has been slower to react and embrace new ways of working. <u>This FAQ series is designed to help the real estate industry better understand (and embrace) e-signatures.</u>

Why haven't they been adopted more widely?
The problem that remains is the validity of electronic signatures - particularly around legislation that requires a document to be "signed" or executed as a deed.

The general approach of the courts has suggested that an electronic signature should satisfy a statutory requirement that something be signed. However, there have also been some curve balls including the decision in Cowthorpe Road 1-1A Freehold Limited v Wahedall where the court was adamant that only pen and paper would suffice.

The Law Commission attempted to provide some clarity on e-signatures in its 2018 consultation. It suggested that an electronic signature is capable of meeting legal requirements where there is an intention to authenticate the document, but sought views on whether legislative reform was necessary to improve confidence in the market and encourage a wider uptake of e-signatures in practice. We await the outcome of that consultation with interest.

Article 4 (249 words)

FAQ E-Signatures in Real Estate: <u>Are e-signatures acceptable in real estate transactions?</u>

Technology is rapidly changing the way in which business is done. Consumers are growing used to an on demand service—whether that is in relation to their banking, shopping or leisure time. Arguably the B2B world, including within real estate, has been slower to react and embrace new ways of working. <u>This FAQ series is designed to help the real estate industry better understand (and embrace) e-signatures.</u>

Are e-signatures acceptable in real estate transactions?
In its 2016 practice note the Law Society acknowledged that the Land Registry and Land Charges Registry required wet-ink signatures on any paper versions of documents sent to them, and HMRC "would normally" expect to stamp a wet-ink version of the document with a wet-ink signature. Essentially this means that any real estate document that does not require registration at the

Land Registry may be suitable for electronic signing and we are finding that our clients are increasingly keen to adopt this technology where possible.

Wholesale adoption of e-signatures across real estate may not, however, be too far off, in the light of the Land Registry's Digital Street initiative. In 2018 it trialled its "sign your mortgage deed" allowing borrowers to digitally sign their mortgage deed online and witnesses no longer needing to be present when the document is signed. This is a progressive move from HM Land Registry and shows its intention to move towards modernising and speeding up real estate transactions.

Article 5 (234 total words)

FAQ E-Signatures in Real Estate: Is e-witnessing permitted?

Technology is rapidly changing the way in which business is done. Consumers are growing used to an on demand service—whether that is in relation to their banking, shopping or leisure time. Arguably the B2B world, including within real estate, has been slower to react and embrace new ways of working. This FAQ series is designed to help the real estate industry better understand (and embrace) e-signatures.

Could e-witnessing be next?

When executing a document as a deed using a sole signatory or swearing a statutory declaration, a witness is required. Might it be possible to witness electronic signatures by video conference or is physical presence always required? We have seen the use of video link to give evidence in court proceedings in a number of cases - could this pave the way for a wider acceptance of remote witnessing?

The Law Commission has suggested that it is "best practice" for the witness to be physically present and in the absence of clear statute or authority on the point the risks will be too great for most to take.

However, we welcome the Land Registry and Law Commission's interest in this subject and are confident that the Law Commission's consultation and its outcomes will encourage more use of e-signatures, paving the way for quicker, safer transactions in real estate and beyond in the years to come.

It took *only 16 words* of main text to convert the first article into the subsequent five—shorter and arguably more digestible—articles. From a return-on-investment perspective, this meant that the addition of *one sentence* generated five times the number of articles and five times the likelihood that a potential client would see a publication from the author. It's worth noting that while the shorter articles satisfy Rule 2 (Short), and drafting the shorter articles would hopefully lead to a greater return on investment, that does not mean that the longer article should not have been (or could not have been) published. As discussed in greater detail in Rule 5 (Recycling and the Rule of Threes), the author could have published the five short articles and then republished each as part of a collection, thus creating a total of six articles from a single work product.

RULE 2: FREQUENTLY ASKED QUESTIONS

Question 1: Can an Article Be Too Short?

Of course—there is always an outer boundary at which an article ceases to be an article. That said, most attorneys would probably be surprised by how short they can make an article and still make it effective, well-received, and capable of generating business.

Consider, for example, the following article:

Privacy FAQ: Does the CCPA apply to personal data about non-Californians (e.g., Europeans)?

No.

Some data privacy laws are designed to apply to personal data collected about individuals that live beyond the country's borders. Most notably, if a company is subject to the general jurisdiction of the European GDPR because it is processing personal data in the context of an establishment within the European Union, the GDPR purports to apply to all personal data—regardless of the residency of the person about whom the data relates. So, for example, if a company processes data in Paris, the GDPR purports to apply to that data regardless of whether the data is about Parisians or Americans. The net result is that if the GDPR attaches it may apply to data subjects "whatever their nationality or place of residence."

The CCPA, on the other hand, applies only to "consumers," a term that is expressly defined as including only "a natural person who is a *California* resident." As a result, if a company processes data in Los Angeles the CCPA applies only to the personal information processed about Californians; it does not apply to information processed about residents of other states or countries.

For attorneys who are used to drafting long newsletters or articles, the preceding might seem uncomfortably short. After all, it is functionally comprised of two paragraphs and has less than 200 words of text. Nonetheless, because it was business practical (see Rule 3: Business Practical) and to the point, it was read four times more than the average article written by an attorney at an Am Law 100 law firm, and 81 percent of its readers were in-house counsel. It was also forwarded, printed, and saved more than 62 times. The takeaway is not to be afraid to publish a short article if you have still provided business-practical content.

Question 2: What If a Topic Is Complex and Needs Greater Length?

Not every topic can be—or should be—dealt with in less than 200 words. Certain issues are simply complex and warrant greater depth and discussion. That does not necessarily mean, however, that you can't write a short article. One of the easiest ways to approach a complex topic is to simply break it up into a series of short, digestible articles that can be published as a series.

For example, if you intend to write an article about how to minimize the likelihood of receiving a civil investigative demand by a particular federal agency, it would not be possible to adequately deal with that issue in 200 words or less. You could, however, break the topic into constituent parts that, individually, are around a page or two. So the article might turn into:

Article 1: Strategies for Avoiding a <<Insert Agency>> Investigation: Part 1 Reviewing your website statements

Article 2: Strategies for Avoiding a <<Insert Agency>> Investigation: Part 2 Monitoring your earnings calls

Article 3: Strategies for Avoiding a <<Insert Agency>> Investigation: Part 3 Flag the agency's top enforcement patterns each quarter

Question 3: Is There Ever a Reason to Do a Long Article?

Yes.

There are exceptions to every rule. So, for example, if you have been invited by a client to coauthor a long publication, you would probably say yes, even if doing so would "violate" Rule 2 (Short). The reason is simple—you have an interest in supporting your clients and growing your relationship with them that is separate and apart from your strategy of how to maximize business development strictly through article writing.

Question 4: If You Do a Series of Short Articles, How Can You Be Sure That a Reader Will Be Able to Find All of Your Content?

As discussed previously, one strategy when drafting short articles is to take a complex concept and divide it into several different—shorter—components. One disadvantage to the practice of serializing content is that all of your substance will not be in a single location and, as a result, the reader may need to hunt around to find all of it. There are several ways that you can address that issue while at the same time following Rule 2. One simple solution is to cross-reference (or link) your articles. So, for example, if you do a multipart series on responding to an agency investigation (see example in Question 2 prior), the conclusion of each short article might contain links to the other articles. Another simple solution is to publish a series of short articles and, after all the articles have been published, repackage the pieces into a single compilation. That method has several benefits. First, the publication of multiple short articles means high return on investment for your publishing time and greater opportunities for name recognition and exposure. The final "compendium" where you republish all of your articles together is a way of repurposing and recycling your content with only a marginal investment of additional time. (See Rule 5: Recycling and the Rule of Threes.)

Rule 2: Reminders

Do	Don't Do
✓ Avoid article formats that are long by design (e.g., law review articles).	✗ Agree to write long articles unless there is an overriding strategic reason to do so.
✓ Steer toward article formats that are short and to the point.	✗ Invest days, weeks, or months into a single article.
✓ Attempt to keep most articles under one or two pages in length.	✗ Assume that a longer article will have more business development impact than a shorter article.
✓ Before embarking upon a longer article, consider the opportunity cost (i.e., how many shorter articles you could write instead).	
✓ Remove superfluous material from your articles.	
✓ Be mindful of your word count and train yourself to think "less is more."	

Rule 2: Worksheet

1. Open the last article that you wrote, perform a word count, and write the word count below: Word Count: _____
2. Reread your article and, in track changes, strike any content that is not necessary.
3. Perform another word count and write the word count below: Word Count: _____   Words Reduced: _____   Percentage Reduction: _____
4. Review your article a second time and see if any additional content can be struck.
5. If your article was originally self-published, republish your revised version and track readership to see if the reduced word count had any impact on the number of reads. If your article was published via a third party (i.e., you do not have the rights to republish it), send both versions of the article to a client, or colleague, and ask them which one they prefer.

CHAPTER 7

Rule 3: Business Practical

No matter how wonderful a sentence is, if it doesn't add new and useful information, it should be removed.

—*Kurt Vonnegut*

One of the most common complaints I hear from in-house counsel about publications is that they tend not to be "business practical." That, of course, begs the question, "What does it mean to be business practical?" The answer is relatively simple. Something is "business practical" if it arms an in-house attorney with something that is actionable, realistic, and beneficial to their business. The challenge, therefore, to an outside counsel who is trying to develop publications that would appeal to and benefit in-house counsel is to make sure that each publication checks some (or all) of these boxes:

- ☑ *Actionable.* Actionable means that an article not only conveys information but also helps the reader understand what specific steps they can or should take in response to the information.
- ☑ *Realistic.* It's one thing to propose an actionable step, but it's another to ensure that the step that you propose is realistic. For example, an article discussing inadvertent waiver of the attorney-client privilege may propose that in-house attorneys should read every e-mail that was sent from their business units to an external party to ensure that a businessperson does not inadvertently forward to third parties advice received from counsel. While that might be an "actionable" step, it certainly would not be a realistic one.

☑ *Beneficial.* At the end of the day, the job of an in-house counsel is to benefit their organization. While there are many ways to benefit an organization, most of the benefits that lawyers provide fall into one of three categories: (1) mitigating corporate risk, (2) decreasing legal costs, or (3) helping to grow revenue. For an article to be beneficial to an in-house attorney, ideally, it should present an action that is realistic to implement and that ties back, in some manner, to risk mitigation, cost reduction, or revenue growth.

If you think that actionable, realistic, and beneficial writing is intuitive to most attorneys, you would be wrong. The traditional "client alert" or "client update" published by most lawyers or law firms is *not* focused on being business practical—it is focused on changes in the law. Indeed, that focus really is the origin of the name "alert"; the article was intended to alert clients about something that changed in the legal landscape. Alerts tend to be interesting to other outside counsel who practice in that space, but if they lack actionable, realistic, and beneficial guidance, they tend not to be business practical and, therefore, of low interest to in-house counsel.

Take for example the following client alert:

U.S. Department of Labor Proposes Changes to Minimum Salary for Overtime Exemptions

On March 7, 2019, the United States Department of Labor issued a notice of proposed rulemaking that would change the minimum salary levels necessary for an employee to be properly classified as exempt from the overtime compensation requirements of the Fair Labor Standards Act. Under the proposed rule, the minimum salary for most exemptions would rise from $455 per week ($23,660 annualized) to $679 per week ($35,308 annualized). The minimum annual compensation for the "highly compensated employee" exemption would rise from $100,000 to $147,414.

For employees in the executive, administrative and professional exemptions, the proposed rule would permit nondiscretionary bonuses and incentive payments (including commissions) to satisfy up to ten percent (10%) of the required minimum salary. In addition, provided that the employee has received at least ninety percent (90%) of the required minimum compensation in each payroll week for 52 weeks, the employer would be permitted to make a single "catch-up" payment within one pay period after the end of the 52-week period, in order to bring the employee's compensation to the required level.

For "highly compensated employees," the proposed rule would require that ten percent (10%) of the minimum annual compensation be paid in the form of a weekly salary, but the remainder could be paid in the form of nondiscretionary bonuses and incentive payments. In addition, the rule would also permit a "catch-up" payment as described above.

The proposed rule would formally rescind the Obama-era rule proposed in 2016, which was blocked by permanent injunction before it could take effect. The proposed rule would make no changes to the duties tests for any of the exemptions.

Once the proposed rule is published in the Federal Register, the public will have 60 days to comment.

While the topic that the alert discusses is theoretically of extremely high interest to a large number of companies (i.e., any company that employs minimum-wage workers), the alert suffers from two main problems. First, it is conveying a news event more than it is providing a substantive discussion. (See discussion of "newscasting" in Rule 4: Shelf Stable.)

Second, it does not include any actionable, realistic, or beneficial advice for the reader. The article talks about a *proposed* change to minimum wages. If you were an in-house labor and employment attorney reading the article, what would you consider the actionable takeaway? Are you supposed to tell your human resources department to increase the wages of exempt employees? Presumably not, as the proposed rule has not been finalized. Are you supposed to warn your human resources department that there is a high likelihood that wages of exempt employees may need to go up and, as a result, the company should begin to prepare? Maybe, but the article does not talk about whether the author believes that the proposed rule is likely to be enacted and, if enacted, when the rule would go into effect. If the salary adjustment would take effect two years after a final rule is enacted, then an in-house attorney would probably not need to put this on the radar of their human resources director. Perhaps an in-house attorney could get ahead of the rule's enactment by preemptively recommending that their company adjust salaries from $23,000 per year to $35,000 per year. Recommending a 52 percent increase in salary to the human resources department as a means of preemptively addressing a rule that has not been enacted, and may never go into force, would not be realistic or beneficial to the company.

The net result is that the article does not offer the reader information that is actionable. To the extent that it implies an action, that action is not realistic and would have questionable benefits to a company.

In many cases, Rule 3 can help you determine whether a topic is worth writing about or if a topic may not be "ripe" to address in an article. In the example above, if there is no business-practical takeaway from the proposed rule, it may be that the topic was not sufficiently ripe to warrant an article.

Rule 3 does not always mean, however, that you don't write about a particular topic. Often it guides *how* you write about the topic. Take for example the following article:

Federal Trade Commission Increases Interlocking Directorate Thresholds for 2019

The Federal Trade Commission has published its annual revision of the interlocking directorate thresholds under Section 8 of the Clayton Act. The new, slightly higher thresholds are effective as of today, March 4, 2019.

Section 8 prohibits a "person" from serving as an officer or director of corporations that compete with one another in the marketplace, except where that competition is very limited. Section 8 also applies where two different individuals represent the same company but serve on competitors' boards.

The existence of an interlock prohibited by Section 8 is a *per se* violation—which means that no defenses may be offered where an illegal interlock is established. It is therefore important to be cognizant of any potential Section 8 issue as well as the current applicable thresholds.

Under the updated thresholds for 2019, a "person" cannot serve as officer or director of any two corporations if:

1. the "capital, surplus, and undivided profits" of each corporation exceed **$36,564,000**; and
2. the corporations are competitors "by virtue of their business and location of operation."

Section 8 does, however, provide exceptions to this general rule. Even where the above elements are satisfied, an interlock is allowed if:

1. the competitive sales of either corporation are less than **$3,656,400**; or
2. the competitive sales of either corporation are less than 2% of the corporation's total sales; or
3. the competitive sales of each corporation are less than 4% of that corporation's total sales.

A Section 8 enforcement action may be brought by the federal antitrust agencies, but there is also a private right of action for Section 8 claims. Companies and individuals should, therefore, keep Section 8 considerations in mind when considering the appointment or undertaking of an officer or director position, and in evaluating current positions.

Unlike the previous example, this article includes an action item for an in-house counsel: consider Section 8 of the Clayton Act when your company is appointing an officer or director. That action item might be made more business practical for an in-house reader, however, by breaking it down into specific action-able steps that are realistic to implement and that have a clear benefit to the company. The article might also apply Rule 3 in the title by signaling to readers that the article will contain business-practical advice. So, for example, consider the following modifications to the title and the addition of a specific action item list:

~~Federal Trade Commission Increases Interlocking Directorate Thresholds for 2019~~ <u>**Three Steps for Avoiding Antitrust Issues When Appointing a New Officer or Director**</u>

> Rule 3: Title changed to signal to readers that the article contains practical action items (i.e., three steps). (Title also changed per Rule 4 to make it shelf stable.)

The Federal Trade Commission has published its annual revision of the interlocking directorate thresholds under Section 8 of the Clayton Act. The new, slightly higher thresholds are effective as of today, March 4, 2019.

. . .

A Section 8 enforcement action may be brought by the federal antitrust agencies, but there is also a private right of action for Section 8 claims. Companies and individuals should, therefore, keep Section 8 considerations

continued

in mind when considering the appointment or undertaking of an officer or director position, and in evaluating current positions.

To avoid the allegation of an interlock, in-house counsel should consider taking the following steps:

1. Require all proposed new officers and directors to complete a questionnaire that includes information regarding any other businesses for which they serve as an officer or director, so that interlocks may be evaluated.
2. Conduct an annual review of whether any current officer or director of your company is also serving as an officer or director of another business that sells competitive goods or products. This may change over time as companies move into competitive markets with each other.
3. Reach out to a member of our team to evaluate any potential interlock, as the law is nuanced and remediation may be needed.

> Rule 3: Three practical action items added.

While the previous example shows how you can make an article business practical by providing specific action items for an in-house counsel to take, there are ways to make an article business practical without telling the reader what to do. One of the easiest approaches is to provide a straightforward answer to a question that in-house attorneys have. Consider the following article:

The Most Frequently Asked Questions About the CCPA: Can a company decide whether to de-identify information or delete information if it receives a 'right to be forgotten' request?

The California Consumer Privacy Act ("CCPA") was enacted in early 2018 as a political compromise to stave off a poorly drafted and plaintiff's friendly ballot initiative. There is a great deal of confusion regarding the requirements of the CCPA given its hasty drafting and lack of detailed legislative history. To help companies understand what the CCPA does, and does not, require, we are publishing a multi-part series that responds to the questions most frequently asked by our clients.

Question: Can a company decide whether to deidentify information or delete information if it receives a 'right to be forgotten' request?

Answer: Yes.

The CCPA states that people have a right to request that a business "delete any personal information about the consumer which the business has collected from the consumer."[1] Although the CCPA does not define what it means to "delete" information or specify how a business must carry out a deletion request, California courts are likely to accept at least two approaches to deletion.

First, a business that receives a deletion request may choose to erase, shred, or irrevocably destroy the entirety of a record that contains personal information. As part of that destruction, any personal information contained within the record will, necessarily, be "deleted."

Second, California courts are likely to accept the anonymization or de-identification of information as a form of deletion. Among other things, a separate California statute (the "California data destruction statute"), which predates the CCPA, requires that businesses take "reasonable steps" to dispose of customer records that "contain[] personal information."[2] That statute recognizes that a customer record can be "dispos[ed]" of without its complete erasure by "modifying the *personal information* within the record to make it unreadable or undecipherable through any means."[3] As a result, if a business maintains a record, but modifies the portion of the record that contains "personal information" (e.g., deletes, redacts, replaces, or anonymizes name, address, Social Security Number, etc.) its actions conform to the California data destruction statute. A strong argument can be made that a business that complies with the destruction standard under the California data destruction statute should be deemed to be in compliance with the deletion requirements of the CCPA, and, as a result, the removal of the portion of a record that contains personal information is sufficient to "delete" such information. This approach is further supported by the fact that the CCPA expressly states that it does not impose any restriction on a business that "retain[s]" information that is "deidentified."[4] As a result if a business de-identifies a record by modifying the personal information within it such that the personal information is no longer associated with an identified individual, the further retention of the record (i.e., the record absent the personal information) is *not* prohibited by the CCPA.[5]

It is worth noting that the use of de-identification or anonymization techniques to remove personal information from a record is also consistent with other California consumer protection statutes. Specifically, in 2015 California enacted a statute that required operators of websites and mobile apps directed towards minors to "remove" content that a minor posted on a website if requested (the California "Erasure Button Law").[6] The Erasure Button Law specifically states that a company is *not* required to "erase or otherwise eliminate" such information if "the operator anonymizes the content or information" such that it "cannot be individually identified."[7]

Notes

1. CCPA § 1798.105(a).
2. Cal. Civ. Code 1798.81.
3. *Id.*
4. CCPA § 1798.145(a)(5).
5. It should be noted that while the California data destruction statute refers to the modification of the personal information so as to make it unreadable, the CCPA defines "deidentified" as meaning that the personal information "cannot *reasonably* identify, relate to, describe, be capable of being associated with or be linked, directly or indirectly, to a particular consumer," so long as the business has processes in place for preventing reidentification attempts. California courts have not indicated whether these two standards diverge.
6. Cal. Bus. & Prof. Code 22581(a)(1).
7. Cal. Bus. & Prof. Code 22581(b)(3).

The preceding article does not contain action items for the reader to take, but it is nonetheless business practical for several reasons.

First, while the article does not contain action items, it is still *actionable*. The structure of the article presents a business question that the reader raised (or that others in a similar position as the reader raised), almost certainly because they were asked the question by their business contacts internally. In the preceding example, the question that the business asked, or may be asking, is simple—are we able to choose to delete or de-identify information if we receive a right-to-be-forgotten request? The article enables the reader to go back to the business with an answer—yes.

Second, the information within the article is realistic in the sense that it provides two methods that a business can utilize to comply with a statute, and both methods—deleting information or removing personal identifiers from information—are practical compliance solutions that most businesses can accomplish.

Third, while the article does not explicitly state the benefit to the reader (or the benefit to the business) of reading the article, given its question-and-answer structure, it arguably does not need to. The benefit of the article is described in the title itself—it answers a question that the reader might have. If the reader is not interested in the question, presumably they will not read the article. If the reader is interested in the question, the benefit is obvious—learning the answer.

The two examples above illustrate another concept. There are ways to structure an article (see Rule 1: Efficient Writing) to functionally force yourself to be business practical. In the first of the two examples above, reworking the title to focus on the three steps to lower a specific risk and then structuring the article to propose three steps almost guaranteed—before the first word of the actual article was written—that the focus of the article would shift from an update to something business practical. In the second of the two examples, drafting a title that focused on a yes-or-no question asked by multiple clients and then providing a yes or a no ensured from the first word that the article would, by nature, be business practical.

One final word when it comes to being business practical. While the ultimate goal is to ensure that the content of your articles is business practical, when it comes to articles, most readers do judge a book by its cover. In other words, it's important to make sure that your title conveys to readers—even before they read your article—that it will contain business-practical content. Consider the following set of articles that was written during the 2020 coronavirus pandemic. Some signaled business-practical content to potential readers; others did not:

Examples of article titles that did *not* signal business practicality

Article Title	Business Practical?
COVID-19 Update— Employee Assistance through Interest-Free Loans	While the content of the article could contain business-practical information (e.g., how companies could offer employees interest-free loans or what risks such loans might involve), it was not clear from the title whether such issues would, or would not, be addressed. Perhaps not surprisingly, the article's readership was relatively low.
The Families First Coronavirus Response Act May Bring (Slightly Modified) Paid Leave to Employees Working for Employers with Fewer Than 500 Employees and to Government Employers	The title indicates that the article would discuss the potential impact of proposed legislation. As discussed above, discussions about potential legislative acts tend not to have business-practical implications. Perhaps not surprisingly, the article's readership was relatively low.
Families First Coronavirus Response Act: Paid Sick Leave Provisions	The title conveys only that it would provide a summary of new legislation. It does not suggest that the summary will contain actionable, realistic, or beneficial information. Perhaps not surprisingly, the article's readership was relatively low.
What Are the Primary Premises Liability Risks Posed by COVID-19?	The title conveys that the article will identify risks but not that it will provide actionable, realistic, or beneficial steps for mitigating those risks. Perhaps not surprisingly, the article's readership was relatively low.

Examples of article titles that *did* signal business practicality

Article Title	Business Practical?
How to Manage Staff during the Coronavirus: Recommendations for HR from a French Perspective	The title indicates that it will provide actionable and beneficial information about managing staff during a time of emergency. Perhaps not surprisingly, the article's readership was nearly twice that of other articles.
Is Covid-19 One "Event": Reinsurance Aggregation	The title indicates that it will provide an answer to a common question that faced many clients during the coronavirus outbreak. Perhaps not surprisingly, the article's readership was nearly four times that of other articles.
Remote Working and COVID-19: How Can I Keep the Wheels Moving on My Real Estate Deals?	The title indicates that it will provide actionable, realistic, and beneficial information about a particular issue (i.e., closing real estate deals). This article illustrates the concept that if a topic is business practical, it does not necessarily matter that the target audience is narrow. In this case, while the article only applied to a niche universe of companies that were involved in real estate transactions at the time of the pandemic, the article's readership was nearly eight times that of other articles.

RULE 3: FREQUENTLY ASKED QUESTIONS

Question 1: Is It Business Practical to Tell a Client They Should Retain You or Your Law Firm?

While you may think that retaining your services is, in fact, the most business-practical solution that any person or company can take to address a problem, recommending that a reader retain your services is not perceived by clients or potential clients as being business practical for a number of reasons.

First, an effective article contains *within it* business-practical solutions. These are solutions that can be implemented just from reading the article. If your solution is that a client should call you for the answer, then in essence all that you have provided is an advertisement for the client to contact you in order to (hopefully) get business-practical advice.

Second, if your article does not contain business-practical advice itself, what would lead a client to suspect that if they contact you directly, your services are going to be business practical?

The best way to develop business through article writing is to *show* a client or potential client the type of business-practical advice that you provide in an article; it gives them a sense and flavor for what you would be like as their attorney. Telling a client to call you for more information or to retain you to provide X, Y, or Z service cheapens your article by turning it into an advertisement and is unnecessary. Clients know that you are available to provide service and know how to contact you without you reminding them.

Question 2: Can Every Article Topic Be Made Business Practical?

No. Some topics simply may not be of practical interest to a business. For example, articles about proposed regulations or legislation are typically not business practical unless, of course, you are a government affairs attorney and your target audience is charged with monitoring proposed legislation.

Question 3: Is Every Academic Topic Not Business Practical?

No. While I generally steer clear of discussing topics that are too academic in nature, it is possible to convert some academic topics into something that is business practical. The trick is to think about what an in-house attorney would want to know about an academic topic, academic discussion, or academic position. For example, if there is an interesting academic debate or symposium taking place, the business-practical angle may be as simple as translating the academic positions taken by policymakers or academics into their business-practical impact. So, for example, if there is a widely discussed academic whitepaper, consider a topic such as "Top Five Ways in Which the <<INSERT>> Paper Is Going to Impact Business."

Question 4: How Can You Tell If a Topic Is Business Practical?

One of the simplest ways for outside counsel to identify business-practical topics is simply to ask yourself what question or issue three or four of your clients have asked you about in the past week. The answer to that question is, almost by definition, a business-practical topic—i.e., it is a question that your clients are currently struggling with and the answer to which would more than likely be viewed as providing immediate business-practical guidance.

Rule 3: Reminders

Do	Don't Do
✓ Signify in your title that the article contains practical action items or advice.	✗ Choose topics that provide information but don't lend themselves to actionable plans.
✓ Include tangible and concrete actions that an in-house attorney can take. Don't be afraid to be direct in suggesting actions like "Consider taking the following steps...."	✗ Choose topics that focus on proposed changes in the law that have not yet been enacted.
✓ Make recommendations that would be realistic for an in-house attorney to implement.	✗ Raise legal problems without offering solutions.
✓ Explain how the action, if taken, will help the business. Consider using introductory phrases such as "To mitigate risk, consider...." or "One step to lower cost might be...."	✗ Report on the state of the law or a development (e.g., a new case, a circuit split, etc.) unless you can tie the new development to a specific action that an in-house attorney can take.
✓ Address real-world questions that clients have about a topic, rather than providing an abstract update on the topic.	
✓ Use an article structure that is inherently business practical insofar as it is designed to offer tangible actions for the reader to take or answer a specific question that the reader is likely to have.	

Rule 3: Worksheet

1. Open the last article that you wrote. Review it to determine if it included business-practical items.

2. If so, write down the specific action items that it suggested that in-house counsel should take or the specific answer to a question posed by in-house counsel:

_____

_____

_____

_____

Were the above action items realistic in the context of the environment in which in-house counsel function? Did they explicitly or implicitly explain how, if they were taken, a company would benefit? If not, rewrite the article and change the actions to make them more realistic and their link to a benefit more explicit.

3. If the article did not provide specific action items, could the article be rewritten to include action items? If so, list some actions that you could suggest here:

_____

_____

_____

_____

If the action items are realistic and would be beneficial, rewrite the article to include the action items.

4. Did the title of your article signal to potential readers that it would contain business-practical information? If not, write a revised title below.

_____

5. If you think that adding new action items or a new title would make the article more business practical, rewrite the article incorporating your answers to questions 2, 3, and 4 and republish it. Track its readership (refer to Rule 6: Metrics) to see if the changes had a positive or negative impact.

6. Practice identifying topics that would and would not appeal to readers by going to Appendix A and identifying, by title, which articles you think would be likely to be most, and least, read.

CHAPTER 8

Rule 4: Shelf Stable

The idea of trying to create things that last—forever knowledge—has guided my work for a long time now.

—Edward Tufte

Most lawyers fall into a trap when it comes to article writing—they look for some current event or new legal development and report on it. That type of article writing is best called "newscasting" as it is more akin to conveying a news headline than providing substantive content. Newscasting lends itself to some common formats of titles (or headlines) that every attorney has seen posted on every law firm's website. They typically start with something like

New 9th Circuit Decision . . .

Government Agency [fill in the four letter acronym] *Publishes Final Report . . .*

Supreme Court Overturns . . .

Congress Enacts Strictest . . .

Attorneys default to newscasting for several reasons, none of which makes for great article writing.

First, new developments are often interesting to *outside counsel*, and, therefore, outside counsel assume that such developments would also be interesting to in-house counsel. That, of course, is not always the case.

Take for example an outside counsel who is neck-deep in a particular legal topic or is involved in defending litigation about a particular issue. That attorney is likely on the lookout for anything that changes the legal landscape and alters their view of the case that they are handling. The problem with that motivation is that, for an article to be effective, it must be important to the intended audience—i.e., in-house counsel or management. While some in-house attorneys might be neck-deep in the same legal issue, the vast majority of them will not be dealing with the topic, and those who are may not be so close to the details as to recognize the importance of the new development.

For example, take the following article: "New York District Court Addresses Mootness Argument in Website Accessibility Case." The article would appeal to an in-house attorney if the week that the article was published, they had a website accessibility case pending in a New York district court. From a marketing standpoint, the intended audience is further narrowed as the author likely wants the article to reach those in-house attorneys who have such a case and have not already selected outside counsel—that may be a null set when it comes to an issue that would only arise after a motion to dismiss is filed.

While an in-house attorney may not be currently dealing with the topic, it is, of course, conceivable (perhaps probable) that they will run into the topic *at some point* in their careers. That is where the concept of shelf stable comes in. If in a year, three years, or five years, an in-house attorney is handling a website accessibility case and is considering whether to raise a mootness argument, will they either find or be enticed to read the above article?

The answer is almost certainly no. The reason is simple. An article that talks about a district court addressing a particular issue is only relevant for a very short amount of time. A year after the article is published, anyone who comes across the article will likely think that the article is stale or that information in the article might be incomplete (at best) or contradicted by new cases or an appeal (at worst). Put differently, the shelf life of the article is limited.

Second, outside counsel default to newscasting when they look around at what their competitors (i.e., other firms) are writing about. One law firm writes about a news event, another law firm writes about the same event, and then a dozen law firms write the same article in order to make sure that they are not left behind. Take for example the following articles, written by different law firms within days of each other:

SEC Proposes Changes to Business, Legal Proceeding and Risk Factor Disclosure Requirements

In Continuing Push toward "Principles-Based" Disclosures, SEC Proposes Additional Amendments to Regulation S-K

SEC Proposes to Modernize Descriptions of Business and Legal Proceedings, and Risk Factor Disclosures, under Regulation S-K

SEC Proposes Changes to Modernize Certain Disclosures under Regulation S-K

Proposed Amendments to Regulation S-K

SEC Proposes Amendments to Regulation S-K: What Foreign Private Issuers Need to Know

SEC Proposes to Modernize Business, Legal Proceedings and Risk Factor Disclosures Required by Regulation S-K

SEC Proposes Amendments to Further Modernize Disclosures under Regulation S-K

Proposed Changes to Regulation S-K Impacting Disclosures

SEC Proposes to Update Disclosures Required by Regulation S-K: Impact on Environmental Disclosure

SEC Proposes to Modernize Business, Legal Proceeding and Risk Factor Disclosure Requirements under Regulation S-K

In total, *hundreds* of law firms wrote *hundreds* of articles on the above topic within a one-week period. Suppose that the pool of securities attorneys to which these law firms were attempting to market consisted of ten thousand attorneys nationwide. Assuming that each in-house attorney read one article on the topic, no firm could expect more than a dozen total reads. Like a news topic that is being reported on the evening news by all news channels simultaneously, there becomes little to differentiate one article from another and there is competition for the limited number of readers. To compound this problem, because most of the articles that were written played on the idea of a new amendment that was just proposed, all of the articles had a limited shelf life. If you were an in-house attorney looking for guidance on Regulation S-K a month, a year, or five years after the above articles were written, in all likelihood you would decide not to read any of them, as reading about what was *proposed* five years earlier would not have much appeal if you were trying to determine what Regulation S-K requires today. The shelf life of these articles was low—at most a month or two.

There is a third reason why lawyers often jump on the newscasting bandwagon. New developments are often topics that land in your lap as an outside counsel. Picture this—a labor and employment attorney wants to write an article but has not decided on a topic. Like manna from heaven, an e-mail arrives from the Equal Employment Opportunity Commission about a recent finding that an employer violated its employees' rights by asking prohibited personal questions on an employment application. Turning that around and sending it to clients in the form of an article can feel like the most obvious way to "check a box" when it comes to article writing. This, of course, leads to the same problems described above. Every outside counsel received the same e-mail from the EEOC, every law firm is considering drafting the same news report, and every article drafted is likely to be viewed as stale within a month.

Regardless of the reason, newscasting is one of the least productive forms of article writing. Topics that are timely are very quickly not timely. In other words, they have a limited shelf life. If articles were items in a supermarket, think of newscasting as selling a fresh tomato. It can be good if purchased in a day or two, but nobody wants to buy the month-old tomato.

When it comes to article writing, your goal should be shelf stability—an article that would appeal to a reader the day that it is published, as well as months, or years, afterward.

From a practical standpoint, this means avoiding some news topics altogether while learning to write about other news topics in a different way.

So which news topics should you avoid? Avoid any news topic that, at its core, has a short shelf life. In the example above, no matter how you spin it, news about an SEC *proposal* can only be relevant until the SEC releases its final rule. In other words, its shelf life is functionally set in stone. Depending on how quickly the SEC releases its rule, that might mean that, at most, it has a year's worth of relevance; in many cases, it might have relevance for as little as 30 days (i.e., the time period in which to comment on the proposed rule).

Not all news topics need to be avoided, however. Some might simply be best approached from a different angle that casts the same information as substance and not news. Consider the following article that was published on March 15, 2019:

NYC Lactation Policies Going into Effect on March 18, 2019

In October 2018, the New York City Council passed two bills, Int. 879-2018 and Int. 905-2018, to supplement existing federal and state laws concerning lactation accommodation policies in the workplace. Currently, New York State Labor Law Section 201-c mandates employers to provide employees with a reasonable number of breaks, and a private sanitary space, other than a restroom, with a chair and flat surface on which to place the breast pump and other personal items, to express breast milk during the workday.

Effective March 18, 2019, Int. 879-2018 requires NYC employers with four or more employees to provide lactation rooms[1] with an electrical outlet, as well as refrigerators, in reasonable proximity to work areas for the purposes of expressing and storing breast milk. Those employers who cannot provide a lactation room, as required under the new law, because of undue hardship are required to engage in cooperative dialogue with affected employees to find a reasonable, alternative accommodation.

The second measure, Int. 905-2018 requires employers to "establish, and distribute to all new employees, policies describing lactation room accommodations, including the process by which an employee can request such accommodation". The policy shall: (1) specify how an employee can submit a request for a lactation room; (2) require the employer to respond to such a request in no later than five (5) business days; (3) provide a procedure to follow when two (2) or more individuals need to use the lactation room at the same time, including the contact information for any follow-up required; (4) state that the employer shall provide reasonable break time for an employee to express breast milk to comply with Section 206-c; and (5) state that if the request for lactation room poses an undue hardship on the employer, the employer shall engage in a cooperative dialogue.[2] Finally, the bill would also require the New York City Commission on Human Rights, in collaboration with the Department

---

continued

of Health and Mental Hygiene, to develop and make available a model lactation room accommodation policy and model request form for employers. The NYC Commission on Human Rights is expected to publish a model lactation accommodation policy on or before March 17, 2019.

Notes

1. If a room designated by an employer to serve as a lactation room is also used for another purpose, the sole function of the room shall be as a lactation room while an employee is using the room to express breast milk. When an employee is using the room to express milk, the employer shall provide notice to other employees that the room is given preference for use as a lactation room.

2. New York City Administrative Code, Section 8-102 requires a "covered entity and a person entitled to, or may be entitled to, an accommodation, to engage in good faith written or oral dialogue concerning the person's accommodation needs; potential accommodations that may address the person's needs, including alternatives to a requested accommodation; and the difficulties that such potential accommodations may pose for the covered entity".

In many ways, this is a quintessential example of newscasting. The week that the article was published, a dozen other law firms wrote similar articles. In addition, as of the day that it was published, the article had—at most—a couple of weeks of shelf life. If you were an HR director who worked in New York City and saw the title of the article after March 18, 2019, just from reading the title—and before investing the time to read the article itself—questions of relevance would start spinning around, like "Did the law ever go into effect?", "I wonder if the New York City Council rescinded the law," "I bet this got amended," or "Maybe I can find an article written this year about the current state of the law." Those immediate reactions drive people away from investing the time to read the article and to understand your expertise in the topic. Not surprisingly, the above article was read only 19 times in six months.

The above topic—i.e., whether employers have to provide female employees with lactation rooms—does not inherently have a short shelf life. In all likelihood, the New York City ordinance that the article discussed will stay on the books for decades, and the article will continue to accurately describe New York law into the indefinite future. This is an example of an article that, if written in a slightly different way, can have a significantly greater impact.

For example, the title of the article can be easily changed so that it does not purport to be discussing a current event and, instead, tries to answer a question that is not time limited. The body of the article also can be modified so that it does not immediately date itself to the reader and, instead, discloses the date of the New York City ordinance in the context of answering a question. The following reworked article removes all indications that the article might have a short shelf life and conveys the same information and the same topic in a shelf-stable manner:

What Do Employers Need to Do to Accommodate Nursing Mothers?

The types of accommodations needed for nursing mothers are governed by state and municipal law, and, therefore, depend on where a company and its offices are based. New York provides a good example of the types of accommodations required under some state laws, and the types of enhancements that some cities push for beyond state minimums. The following shows the requirements under state law, as well as the requirements that apply to most employers that have four or more employees and an office in New York City:

Requirement	New York State[1]	New York City[2]
Reasonable amount of breaks	✓	✓
Private sanitary space other than a restroom (with a chair and a flat surface on which to place a breast pump)	✓	✓
Electrical outlet	✗	✓
Refrigerators for storing milk	✗	✓
Written policy describing lactation room accommodations	✗	✓

Employers that are considering drafting a lactation accommodation policy should consider including the following items:

1. Specify how an employee can submit a request for a lactation room;
2. Indicate that the employer is to respond to such a request in no later than five (5) business days;

---

continued

> 3. Provide a procedure to follow when two (2) or more individuals need to use the lactation room at the same time, including the contact information for any follow-up required;
> 4. State that the employer shall provide reasonable break time for an employee to express breast milk;
> 5. State that, if the request for a lactation room poses an undue hardship on the employer, the employer shall engage in a cooperative dialogue.
>
> **Notes**
> 1. New York State Labor Law § 2016-c.
> 2. New York City Council Int. 0879-2018, Int. 905-2018.

In this case, the numbers prove the point. The second version of the article was released four months after the statute that it discussed went into effect. Because the article was not tied to the news event, it did not have to compete for readership against other articles that came out at the time of the statute's passage. Also because it was not tied to the news event, it has a near-unlimited shelf life. An HR director who came upon the article the week it was published and one who came upon the article a year after it was published would be equally likely to read the article for its content. The expanded shelf life led to a ten times increase in readership.

The takeaway from Rule 4 is not to avoid newscasting at all costs. It's simply to consider, as part of a business development strategy, going beyond newscasting. For example, the original article above may have been written in the manner it was, and on the date that it was, for a good reason. Perhaps existing clients would expect to be alerted about a new regulation. Or there might have been a compliance deadline that meant it was important that clients realized that the article should be read that day, about an event that was to occur that month, in order to avoid liability. If you are going to publish an article that amounts to newscasting in order to satisfy a specific purpose or need, however, consider republishing the article with the same content but written in a shelf-stable form. The former version may serve the purpose of alerting clients to the news in a timely manner; the latter version serves the separate purpose of creating a shelf-stable resource with long-tail marketability. Publishing the same content twice also has the added benefit of double exposure (see Rule 5: Recycling and the Rule of Threes).

RULE 4: FREQUENTLY ASKED QUESTIONS

Question 1: Should All Articles That You Write Be Shelf Stable?

Not necessarily.

In Section III, I discuss "deviating from the rules" and recognize that all rules are meant to be broken even when it comes to article writing. There are many situations in which you may decide that you should write an article that is not shelf stable. Where such a decision is based upon a weighing of the benefits of writing the shelf-limited article against the benefits of writing a shelf-stable article, it is likely the "right" decision.

Question 2: What Are Some Examples of Situations in Which You Might Consider Writing a Shelf-*Limited* Article?

One situation in which a shelf-limited article might be warranted would be if there is a news event of overarching importance such that your clients would expect that you, as an expert in your field, at a minimum acknowledge the event or at a maximum provide guidance about it. In those situations, it may make sense to write an article. When doing so, however, it's important to realize that the benefit of the article is largely to communicate with your existing clients about the news event, not necessarily to attract new clients. In other words, realize that if the news event (e.g., pandemic, war, natural disaster, etc.) is of high visibility, prospective clients are likely to be inundated with articles written by others and, as a result, are unlikely to see your writing.

Question 3: Do Clients Sometimes Expect You to Write on a Current Event?

Yes. As I mentioned in the previous paragraph, there are certain events for which existing clients expect a communication from their attorneys about the impact of a particular event. If your clients expect the update, it may make sense to provide it to them so, at a minimum, they receive your perspective about the current event without seeking out the perspective of others. While these types of articles may make sense, their lack of shelf stability means that they may have a more limited impact than many of the other articles that you write.

When thinking about whether to write about a current event, it's important to remember not to let the exception swallow the rule. While there are absolutely current events that your clients may expect you to communicate about, I have found that those tend to be few and far between and involve events that are truly out of the ordinary. Outside counsel tend to overassume that certain events rise to the level of needing to be reported. To put it in context, in a typical year I find that there may be, at most, one or two situations in which a current event necessitates an article.

Question 4: Is There a Way to Write about a Current Event and Be Shelf Stable?

Yes. I have found that in almost every situation there is a way to structure an article to be shelf stable. From a pedagogical standpoint, before writing about a current event, try to step back and ask yourself what is the underlying impact that the event is having in your area of law and *what other types of current events* might have the same impact. Once you answer that question, think about writing your article for the *type* of event (or the type of impact that the event has) rather than writing about the event itself.

To provide an example, if you are a labor and employment attorney and are considering writing about the impact of a specific natural disaster upon the obligation of employers to continue to pay their employees, if you wrote an article titled "Hurricane Nancy: Do companies have to pay employees who can't come to work because they have been flooded?", it would have a very short shelf life. You could write the exact same article but, by focusing on the type of event (as opposed to the specific event), you could broaden its applicability. So, for example, simply by titling your article "Disruptions from Hurricanes: Do companies have to pay employees who can't come to work because they have been flooded?", you have made it shelf stable (it now applies to *any* disruption caused by a hurricane, not just the disruption caused by a specific hurricane on a specific date). You might want to consider broadening it even further to talk about the type of impact that an event has. For example, the same article could be retitled as "Do you have to pay employees who can't come to work because of a natural disaster?" The last title is shelf stable (i.e., it would be relevant to an in-house counsel dealing with Hurricane Nancy, Hurricane George, or any other to-be-named hurricane), has broad applicability (i.e., it also applies to tornados, tsunamis, earthquakes, fires, etc.), and it is business practical as it answers a specific business-related question (Rule 3: Business Practical).

Question 5: Does an Article Have to Be Timeless in Order to Be Shelf Stable?

Timeless is a tall order!

If you asked an attorney from the 1800s what topic they thought had a long shelf life, they might say something like "the implications of tort liability when a servant is injured by a horse and buggy." That topic probably was shelf stable in the 1800s and might have been relevant for a hundred years but would mean very little today.

Don't make your criterion for meeting Rule 4 whether an article is timeless but rather whether it has no definitive expiration date. If you have to assign a time value to it as a mental exercise, ask yourself whether there is any reason why the article might be out of date in five years. If the answer is yes, consider writing on another topic (or restructuring your article so that the answer can be no). If the answer is no (i.e., you think that the article would be just as relevant in five years), don't worry about the possibility that something unexpected might happen in the world that could cause the article, or the substance of the article, to be out of date before then.

Rule 4: Reminders

Do	Don't Do
✓ Pick topics that summarize the law.	✗ Write on enforcement actions of federal or state agencies, unless the topic of the article is about the substantive principle upheld and *not* about the agency's action.
✓ Pick topics that analyze a legal question or issue that your target audience is likely to have.	
✓ Pick topics that are likely to be reoccurring questions.	✗ Write about upcoming events.
✓ Pick topics that answer a legal or factual question.	✗ Write about proposed legislation.
✓ Pick topics that are not likely to be radically altered by the outcome of an anticipated event.	✗ Write about proposed rulemakings.
	✗ Write about how a single court has come out on an issue (unless it's the Supreme Court).

Rule 4: Worksheet

1. Write down the titles of your last three articles: Article 1: _____ Article 2: _____ Article 3: _____
2. If any of your titles include dates, or references to current events, consider whether you can change the titles to remove the date or event so that a reader would perceive the article as being accurate whether it is read today or five years from now.
3. If any of your titles include temporal terms that implicitly anchor your article to a point in time (e.g., "court *just* issued," "*proposed* rule," "*upcoming* decision"), consider whether you can change the title to remove the implicit temporal reference.
4. Review the body of your articles and remove any explicit reference to dates or move such references to footnotes.
5. If one of the articles that you listed has a date, a reference to a current event, or a temporal term that *cannot* be removed without negating the entirety of the article, consider whether the readership of the article at the time that it was published was sufficient to justify the time that you invested to draft the article.
6. If you modified any article above to remove a date, a reference to a current event, or a temporal term, consider republishing the article, tracking its readership, and comparing the readership to that of the original publication.

CHAPTER 9

Rule 5: Recycling and the Rule of Threes

There's nothing new under the sun—you just get a can of paint out.

—*Robert Plant*

My number one pet peeve is inefficiency. I remember when I realized that. I was a junior associate asked to write a section of an appellate brief. I jumped onto Lexis, researched the issue at hand, and found what looked like the perfect 50-page-long case. I printed it out and began to read.

Ten minutes in, something dawned on me—I knew how the case came out. Why? I had read the same case, on the same topic, six months earlier. Of course, knowing how the case came out did me no good at the time. I still had 40 more pages to go to find the right quotes that I needed for my brief and to flag the issues that might be raised by the respondent. As I read the case from start to finish, I had intermittent feelings of frustration and guilt. Frustration because, in some trash pile somewhere, there was a fully underlined, highlighted, flagged, and annotated version of the case from six months earlier, prepared by none other than me. Guilt because I was billing my client hours of time for something that could have taken ten minutes if I just had my earlier research.

From that day forward, efficiency has been one of my top priorities. If you walked into my office, you would see a row of bookshelves that house hundreds of personal research files on virtually every substantive topic I have advised on over the years. Each research file contains printouts of underlined, highlighted, flagged, and annotated cases, agency decisions, rules, and regulations. Needless to say, I don't bill clients to research a topic that I've already driven to ground.

I try to strike out inefficiency when it comes to article writing as well. What does inefficiency mean in the context of article writing? It's simple. If an article will only have one life—i.e., one publication or one purpose—it's inefficient to spend time drafting it. Indeed, I've gotten to the point where, if an article will only have two purposes, it's still too inefficient to invest the time to draft it. At a bare minimum, before I put pen to paper (or finger to keyboard), a publication must have *at least* three different uses.

The following illustrates how the "Rule of Threes" works.

In 2015, I decided to write a series of articles on data privacy and data security. Based upon the Rule of Threes, however, I wanted to make sure that if I invested the time to write, each article would be used a minimum of three times.

I decided that I would create a consistent structure for each of the articles (see Rule 1: Efficient Writing). My plan was that each of the articles would be published in a standalone form, and, later, because the articles used a consistent structure, they would be collected together and published as a cohesive compilation.

For example, in 2015, I published the following article on privacy notices (Use No. 1):

What In-House Counsel Need to Know About Website Privacy Notices

Although financial institutions, healthcare providers, and websites directed to children are required to create consumer-privacy policies under federal law, other types of websites are not. In 2003, California became the first state to impose a general requirement that most websites post a privacy policy.

Under the California Online Privacy Protection Act ("CalOPPA"), all websites that collect personal information about state residents must post an online privacy policy if the information is collected for the purpose of providing goods or services for personal, family, or household purposes. Since the passage of the CalOPPA, most websites that collect information—whether or not they are directed at California residents or are otherwise subject to the CalOPPA—have chosen to post an online privacy policy.

Relevant Facts		
10 minutes: Average time it takes for a person to read a privacy policy.	244 hours: Amount of time it would take a person to read the privacy policies of all the unique websites they visit in a year.	$0.59: Premium that study participants were willing to pay to purchase a $15 item from a website that proactively displayed strong privacy protections instead of from one with no privacy position.[1]

1. Janice Tsai et al., *The Effect of Online Privacy Information on Purchasing Behavior: An Experimental Study*, 6TH WORKSHOP ON THE ECONOMICS OF INFORMATION SECURITY (WEIS) (June 2007), http://www.econ infosec.org/archive/weis2007/papers/57.pdf.

Factors counsel should consider when drafting or reviewing a privacy policy:

1. Is the organization subject to a federal law that requires a privacy policy to take a particular form or include particular information?
2. Does the privacy policy describe the main ways in which the organization collects information?
3. Does the privacy policy describe the ways in which the organization shares information with third parties?
4. Does the privacy policy discuss data security? If so, is the level of security indicated appropriate?
5. Would the privacy policy interfere with a possible merger, acquisition, or sale of the organization's assets?
6. Would the privacy policy interfere with future ways in which the organization may want to monetize data?
7. Does the privacy policy use terms that might be misunderstood or misinterpreted by a regulator or a plaintiffs' attorney?
8. Does the privacy policy comply with the laws in each jurisdiction to which the organization is subject (e.g., CalOPPA)?
9. Should the privacy policy only govern information collected via the organization's website or all information collected by the organization?
10. Does the privacy policy appropriately disclose and discuss network marketing and behavioral advertising?
11. Does the privacy policy need to discuss the tracking that the organization may conduct of its clients or website visitors?
12. Could the privacy policy be understood by the average person?
13. Can the privacy policy be easily viewed on a smartphone or a mobile device?
14. Does the policy provide information to users concerning how they can contact the organization about privacy-related questions or complaints?
15. Does the policy discuss what information may be modified or changed by a user?

In 2016, after publishing a number of other articles using a similar structure, I published all of the articles as a compilation in a 67-page Contemporary Legal Note for the Washington Legal Foundation titled *Data Privacy and Security: A Practical Guide for In-House Counsel* (Use No. 2):

Because all of the topics in the guide were shelf stable (see Rule 4: Shelf Stable), they remained just as relevant in 2017 as they did when they were originally written in 2015. So I decided to publish them again. Of course, the law had changed slightly in the intervening years, so I reviewed and updated each topic to account for changes in the law and then reverse serialized (i.e., republished) each article. The following was republished in 2017 (Use No. 3). The underlined text shows the new content:

What In-House Counsel Need to Know About Website Privacy Notices (2017)

Although financial institutions, health care providers, and websites directed to children are required to create consumer privacy policies under federal law (see, e.g., section discussing collecting information from children), other types of websites are not. In 2003, California became the first state to impose a general requirement that most websites post a privacy policy.

Under the California Online Privacy Protection Act ("CalOPPA"), all websites that collect personal information about state residents must post an online privacy policy if the information is collected for the purpose of providing goods or services for personal, family, or household purposes.[1] Since the passage of the CalOPPA, most websites that collect information— whether or not they are directed at California residents or are otherwise subject to the CalOPPA—have chosen to post an online privacy policy. The California Attorney General published a form that allows consumers to report potential violations of CalOPPA online. This online reporting tool will increase California's ability to identify and notify entities in violation of CalOPPA.

On January 1, 2016, Delaware followed suit by enacting the Delaware Online Privacy and Protection Act ("DOPPA"). Similar to CalOPPA, DOPPA requires that website and app operators that collect personally identifiable information of Delaware residents conspicuously post a comprehensive privacy policy and conform to other privacy related requirements.

Relevant Facts			
2 Number of states that require operators of websites that collect PII to disclose a privacy policy.	10 minutes: Average time it takes for a person to read a privacy policy.	244 hours: Amount of time it would take a person to read the privacy policies of all the unique websites they visit in a year.	$0.59: Premium that study participants were willing to pay to purchase a $15 item from a website that proactively displayed strong privacy protections instead of from one with no privacy position.

What to think about when drafting or reviewing a privacy policy:

1. Is your organization subject to a federal law that requires that a privacy policy take a particular form, or include particular information?
2. Does the privacy policy describe the main ways in which your organization collects information?
3. Does the privacy policy describe the ways in which your organization shares information with third parties?
4. Does the privacy policy discuss data security? If so, is the level of security indicated appropriate?
5. Would the privacy policy interfere with a possible merger, acquisition, or sale of your organization's assets?
6. Would the privacy policy interfere with future ways in which your organization may want to monetize data?
7. Does the privacy policy use terms that might be misunderstood or misinterpreted by a regulator or a plaintiff's attorney?
8. Does the privacy policy comply with the laws in each jurisdiction in which your organization is subject (*i.e.*, CalOPPA or DOPPA)?

9. Should the privacy policy only govern information collected via your organization's website or all information collected by your organization?
10. Does the privacy policy appropriately disclose and discuss network marketing and behavioral advertising?
11. Does the privacy policy need to discuss the tracking that your organization may conduct of its clients or website visitors?
12. Could the privacy policy be understood by the average person?
13. Can the privacy policy be easily viewed on a smartphone or a mobile device?
14. Does the policy provide information to users concerning how they can contact your organization about privacy related questions or complaints?
15. Does the policy discuss what information may be modified or changed by a user?

Note

1. CAL. BUS. & PROF. CODE § 22575 et seq.

The "cost" in terms of time and effort of the additional publication was 102 new words.

The updated articles were again collected into a compilation that was separately published in 2017 as *Data Privacy and Security: A Practical Guide for In-House Counsel 2017 Edition* (Use No. 4). The process of reverse serialization was repeated in 2018 (Use No. 5), as was the process of creating a compilation for 2018 (Use No. 6).

All in all, the initial article that I drafted in 2015 was recycled and reused six times. From a readership and visibility perspective, while the first publication in 2015 reached a couple hundred readers, by publishing the compilations and updated versions, the article reached thousands of in-house counsel.

While the example above involved uses that were all publications, that does not have to be the case. There are many different "uses" of an article, only some of which relate to publication. Consider the following possible uses:

1. a first publication as a standalone article;
2. a second publication as a collection or compilation of articles on a similar topic;
3. a third publication as an updated article;
4. an insert in or basis for a presentation;

5. an answer to a client question; or

6. a section of a book.

To provide a second example of how recycling and the Rule of Threes can work in practice, in 2018, I published a "Frequently Asked Questions" series that included an article that addressed a similar topic concerning website privacy notices. The following was one of the questions published (Use No. 1):

Privacy FAQ: Does the California Consumer Privacy Act require that a retailer provide a privacy policy "at or before" the point at which information is collected?

No.

A privacy policy typically discloses the following information to the public:

- The categories of information collected from a consumer directly and from third parties about a consumer,
- The purpose for which information is collected and used,
- The extent to which the business tracks or monitors consumers,
- The extent to which the business shares the consumer's information with third parties,
- The standard by which the business protects the information from unauthorized access,
- The ability (if any) of a consumer to request access to their information,
- The ability (if any) of a consumer to request the deletion of their information,
- The ability (if any) of a consumer to request the rectification of inaccurate information, and
- The process by which a business will inform consumers about changes in its privacy practices.

The California Consumer Privacy Act only requires that a business that collects a consumer's personal information disclose the *first two* categories above, and that the disclosure be "at or before the point of collection." While this may seem like a technical difference, it does *not* require that *all* of the information contained in a privacy notice be disclosed at that time. As a result, if a retailer discloses the categories of information collected and the purpose of the collection to its consumers orally, contextually, or in a summary form, at or before the point of collection, the CCPA does not mandate that the entirety of a privacy notice be provided to the consumer "at or before" the point of collection. A retailer could, for example, disclose contextually that it collects credit cards from a consumer (by asking for their credit card), and disclose the purpose for the collection (e.g., that it will be charging their credit card) and it arguably would be in full compliance with the California Act without ever delivering a privacy notice.

Because this was a frequently asked question among my clients, I was certain that the question posed in the article would soon be asked by another client. Not surprisingly, within a week, a client sent the following request:

From: John Smith

To: Zetoony, David

Subject: In-store Privacy Notice

David,

We have heard that we need to distribute our privacy notice whenever we collect personal information and are exploring delivering our California Consumer Privacy Act privacy policy by email for those customers who are providing personal information at the register in our stores. The emails would be delivered simultaneously upon collection of the customer email or very shortly thereafter. Can you provide some guidance in this area? Are we required to send every person that checks out our full privacy notice?

Best Regards,

John

Having a publication directly on topic allowed for a quick, thorough, and well-reasoned response. The client received an hour's worth of analysis but only paid for a few minutes for me to modify and transmit the following e-mail (Use No. 2):

From: David Zetoony

To: John Smith

Subject: In-store Privacy Notice

John,

There is a lot of confusion about the California Consumer Privacy Act. While many law firms have been reporting that it requires stores to provide a privacy notice to customers, it does *not* state that.

In terms of context, a privacy policy typically discloses the following information to the public:

- The categories of information collected from a consumer directly and from third parties about a consumer,
- The purpose for which information is collected and used,
- The extent to which the business tracks or monitors consumers,
- The extent to which the business shares the consumer's information with third parties,
- The standard by which the business protects the information from unauthorized access,
- The ability (if any) of a consumer to request access to their information,
- The ability (if any) of a consumer to request the deletion of their information,
- The ability (if any) of a consumer to request the rectification of inaccurate information, and
- The process by which a business will inform consumers about changes in its privacy practices.

The California Consumer Privacy Act only requires that a business that collects a consumer's personal information disclose the *first two* categories above, and that the disclosure be "at or before the point of collection." While this may seem like a technical difference, it does *not* require that *all* of the information contained in a privacy notice be disclosed at that time. As a result, if you disclose the categories of information collected and the purpose of the collection to your consumers orally, contextually, or in a summary form, at or before the point of collection, the CCPA does not mandate that the entirety of the privacy notice be provided to the consumer "at or before" the point of collection. You could, for example, disclose contextually that you are collecting credit cards from a consumer (by asking for their credit card), and disclose the purpose for the collection (e.g., that you will be charging their credit card) and you arguably would be in full compliance with the California Act without ever delivering your privacy notice.

In essence, the second use was to provide an efficient and direct response to a client for a fraction of the time (and cost) that it would otherwise have taken to research and respond. In this case, the article was also republished as part of a compiled collection of FAQs on the referenced statute (Use No. 3).

RULE 5: FREQUENTLY ASKED QUESTIONS

Question 1: Is There a Limit to How Many Times Content Can Be Recycled?

Not really.

You obviously do not want to be publishing the same article over and over each week. That said, there is really no limit to how often you can reuse content. That is even more true when some of the uses are not tied to publications (e.g., responding to client questions). Even in the context of publications, so long as the topic remains relevant and the article is written in a shelf-stable manner, it can be updated and republished every year as part of an annual series.

Question 2: Can You Recycle Material That You Learned While Providing Advice to a Client?

Yes.

Most of what we learn as outside counsel comes while we are responding to a particular inquiry or question from a client. While of course you would never publish any privileged information that you receive from a client (e.g., whether a law applies to a client, a client's product, or a client's services), to the extent that you develop knowledge as part of a client engagement, and that knowledge has broader applicability to other companies, consider repurposing it and sharing it more generally.

Question 3: If You Publish the Same Content Three Times, Won't Clients Identify the Information as Stale?

No.

The Rule of Threes is not about publishing the same article week after week. If you decide to reuse an article by republishing it, there are several steps that you can take to help ensure that the article is not perceived as stale or repetitive.

For example, if you are going to republish an article close in time to the original publication, consider publishing the article to a different audience that would be unlikely to have seen your first publication. Alternatively you could tailor the article to a new audience by adding an introduction or a conclusion that applies the content of the article to a particular industry or use case.

If you are going to republish an article after a period of time has elapsed (e.g., a year), most of your new readers will not have read the first publication. Those who did read your first publication are likely to have forgotten about it or may be interested in rereading it to see if your analysis, viewpoint, or conclusions changed over time. Sometimes publishing the same article year over year is valuable to your readers in and of itself as the latest "edition" of the article signals to them that the content is still timely, valid, and accurate.

Question 4: Can Any Article Be Republished and Recycled?

Yes and no.

Almost every article can be republished and recycled *if* it was initially written in a manner that promotes republishing and recycling. What does that mean? If the structure of the article followed a formula (Rule 1: Efficient Writing), and the article was originally designed to be shelf stable (Rule 4: Shelf Stable), then there is a 99 percent chance that it can be reused and recycled even if the only recycling is republishing the revised and updated article the following year. If, on the other hand, you didn't consider recycling at the time that you originally published the article such that its structure may not be conducive to reuse and its topic has a short shelf life, it may not be recyclable. So, for example, if you wrote a time-dependent newscasting article (which would, of course, violate Rule 4: Shelf Stable), it is unlikely that it could be recycled at a later date. If the formula for the article was not such that it permitted easy reuse in terms of client advice (which might violate Rule 1: Efficient Writing), it is unlikely that it could be recycled for a different purpose even as of the date it was published.

In terms of making this concept tangible, consider the following title of an article that was published during the first month of the coronavirus outbreak in 2020:

The First Virtual Trial in the Commercial Court in Spite of COVID 19

The above article consisted of a case commentary and description of a hearing that was conducted on March 19, 2020, in the United Kingdom. The article itself followed no formula and consisted of an abstract summary. As a result, it "violated"

Rule 1. The topic was shelf limited almost to the week of March 19, 2020, as the article was out of date almost immediately once there was a second virtual trial. Trying to republish or recycle this article would have been nearly impossible.

Had the authors considered recycling and the Rule of Threes, they might have chosen to draft a very different article that was amenable to recycling. For example, consider the following title that could have been written about the same event:

How to Ask For, and Receive, a Virtual Trial in a Commercial Court during a National Crisis

The above topic might have been recycled numerous times, including as

1. a response to any client who, during the coronavirus outbreak, was also interested in seeking a virtual trial,
2. a response to any client who, during a future pandemic or national emergency, was considering a virtual trial, and
3. a new publication during the next national emergency (whether caused by pandemic, natural disaster, strike, etc.).

Question 5: At Some Point, Should You Stop Recycling Content? Yes.

Every topic (and article) has a half-life. If you have followed Rule 4 (Shelf Stable), then the half-life of your article will not be days or weeks but years. That said, at some point in time the topic will no longer be of interest to readers either because the law has changed, the facts underlying the issue have changed, or the information contained in the article is well accepted and no longer necessitates an article. Consider, for example, an article written in 1980 about piracy tied to recording television shows on a VHS player. That article might have had a good ten-year run, but today's audience would not know what a VHS player is (and may not even understand why someone would want to record a television program instead of just replaying it from a streaming service).

The next chapter—Rule 6: Metrics—will discuss how to monitor your articles' readership. That monitoring can help, among other things, identify when a particular article or topic has reached its half-life and might need to be retired or substantially updated.

Rule 5: Reminders

Do	Don't Do
✓ Consider article topics that are conducive to being updated and republished. Prefer long-lasting article topics to those that have a short shelf life (see also Rule 4: Shelf Stable). ✓ When considering your article structure (see also Rule 1: Efficient Writing), think about whether the structure that you choose can be repurposed as a compilation or broken apart and sent out as a serial publication. ✓ When considering your article structure (see also Rule 1: Efficient Writing), think about whether the structure, tone, and style would allow you to leverage the content in order to quickly and efficiently respond to client questions on the same topic. ✓ If you intend to write several articles, cluster the topics around a similar theme with the intention of compiling the individual articles into a cohesive collection that can be republished.	✗ Use article topics that have a short shelf life (see Rule 4: Shelf Stable) and, therefore, will be difficult to repurpose in the future. ✗ Use different article structures every time you write, as those differences will make it difficult or impossible to create compilations or merge topics to create future publications. ✗ Write for publications that require you to convey the copyright of your work to a third party or that prohibit you from republishing or reprinting your article.

Rule 5: Worksheet

1. Write down the topic of an article that you would like to write: Topic: _____
2. Identify three uses that you intend to make of the publication: Use No. 1: _____ Use No. 2: _____ Use No. 3: _____ If you have difficulty identifying three uses, change the topic of your article to something different and try again.
3. What article format or structure do you need to use in order to allow the article to "work" for all three purposes?
4. Write the article for Use No. 1.
5. After the article is written, apply it to Use No. 2. How much additional time did it take to repurpose it for Use No. 2?
6. After the article is written, apply it to Use No. 3. How much additional time did it take to repurpose it for Use No. 3?

CHAPTER 10

Rule 6: Metrics

With a metric you can really go to town, otherwise it is just abstract nonsense.

—*Jennifer Tour Chayes*

Over the course of my career, I have been fortunate enough to know many brilliant attorneys. Some of them are fantastic writers in certain contexts. For example, they can put together cohesive and articulate appellate briefs in days that would take others (including me) weeks. When it comes to publishing articles, these same writers often flounder or fail. For years I couldn't figure out how someone could excel in writing in one context and yet struggle in another.

It turns out that the answer is relatively straightforward.

Almost all people learn through feedback loops. They try something—a new technique, a new style, or a new approach. If it works, then they know to replicate or build upon the new technique in the future. If it does not work, then they learn over time to avoid the behavior. The more immediate and transparent a feedback loop, the faster someone learns. So, for example, if you are learning for the first time how to drive a stick shift and try to shift into second gear but immediately hear a horrendous grinding sound, you know you've done something wrong. It may take several tries, but if you always hear a loud grind every time you do it wrong, it does not take too long to learn to avoid the sound by timing the clutch.

Now imagine that you take away the feedback. Every time you try to shift gears, you don't hear anything, i.e., you can't tell whether it was a smooth transition or you ground the gears. It would be nearly impossible to learn to drive. You would simply keep making the same mistakes over and over and either believe that you were doing it right or believe that you were doing it wrong. In the former situation you would keep trying fruitlessly (until the transmission eventually broke); in the latter situation you would eventually give up.

When it comes to writing publications for business development, many authors find themselves without an effective feedback loop. They put together an article that may, or may not, follow the rules discussed in this book and send it out into the world. They believe that the only feedback loop is whether the article turns into business (i.e., they receive a new client, they are retained for a new project, etc.). The problem with using new projects as a feedback loop is that it may take many articles to build an expertise-based reputation. New projects may come months, or years, after an article is published, and when a project comes in, it may not be immediately obvious that it was the result of a publication. It would be like learning to drive a stick shift by hearing the grinding sound days—instead of seconds— after you shifted. New engagements are simply not immediate or transparent enough to provide an effective feedback loop. Without something more immediate and more descriptive, it's extremely difficult for attorneys to learn from their publications and evolve their writing to be more effective over time.

Luckily, in this day and age, there is no shortage of data and metrics about readership that can provide immediate feedback concerning the interest others have in your publications and the amount of brand recognition that your publications generate. You simply need to know where to find it.

Almost every digital publication collects some form of data that an author can use to gauge the success of their articles. For example, if you self-publish articles through your law firm's website, chances are that your firm utilizes analytics cookies. Analytics cookies are small snippets of code that are placed on the browser of a visitor to a website for the purpose of tracking their behavior. They are typically free for websites to use and, among other things, can provide information such as the total number of people who visited your article, where those people came from geographically, how long they spent reading your article, and whether they interacted with any of its contents. Some analytics cookies go further and provide demographic information (e.g., age, business, etc.) of the visitors.[1]

If you publish articles through the major social media channels, those too provide—at no cost—analytics. For example, LinkedIn provides the number of views, reactions, comments, or times that an article is reshared on their platform.

When it comes to legal publications, there are several legal-industry-specific services that aggregate articles across law firms and practitioners and republish them to in-house counsel. Three of the most popular legal publication aggregation services are JDSupra, Lexology, and Mondaq. These services often provide useful analytics with differing degrees of granularity for attorneys or law firms that subscribe to their service. For example, authors who subscribe to Lexology receive the number of times that an article has been read on the Lexology platform and the number of "unique users" who have read the article:

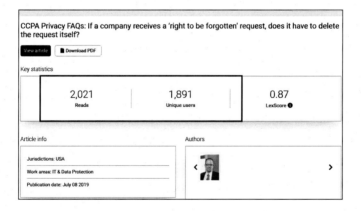

---

1. Note that in some jurisdictions, such as the European Union, a website may be required to ask visitors to consent before placing analytics cookies. As a result, and to the extent that you decide to use visitors to your own website as a metric for benchmarking, make sure that your website complies with all laws that regulate tracking of individuals online or the placement, or reading, of cookies on web visitors' browsers.

Authors can also access information regarding the specific companies that accessed an article, the geographic location of the readers, and the interactions of users (e.g., was the article printed, forwarded, saved, etc.?).

While there are pros and cons to the readership metrics provided by each legal aggregation service, and none paint the full picture of the exposure that an article has garnered, any of them can serve as a proxy for how well an article has been distributed and can help form the basis of a feedback loop that can improve and hone writing.

The first step in utilizing metrics is to find a simple consistent metric against which you intend to judge the penetration of your articles. In some respects, the accuracy and precision of the metric you choose is less important than identifying a metric that is easy for you to consistently check for most of your publications.

The second step in utilizing metrics is to force yourself to check your chosen metric methodically. For example, if you are publishing on a weekly basis, you should be checking the metrics of your articles also on a weekly basis. If you are publishing on a daily basis, you should be checking the metrics of your recent articles daily. Remember, for metrics to serve as an effective feedback loop, they must be immediate (or as close in time to publication as possible). One easy trick is to download your source of metrics as a link either on the desktop of your smartphone or as a homepage in your web browser. If your metrics load every time you boot up your computer or glance at your phone, you can ensure that you are receiving feedback constantly concerning your publications.

The third step is to compare and contrast. See which of your articles had higher and lower readership. If the metrics to which you have access provide granular data concerning readers' engagement and interactions with your articles, see which of your articles garnered more user interaction or longer dwell times. As you develop more articles (and hence more data points), trends will start to emerge. You will find that certain types of articles are more popular than others. Sometimes those trends confirm suspicions that you may have had about what topics might be popular with clients. Other times trends will uncover areas that you had assumed would be uninteresting or that might have been obvious to you but were not obvious to readers.

The fourth step is to draw testable hypotheses from the data. If your shorter articles seem to be read, printed, forwarded, or shared more often than your longer articles, your hypothesis might be that your readership will increase if you steer more of your articles to a short format. If articles that you thought were timely and extremely interesting are not resonating with readers, you might start to consider shifting future articles to another topic. With a feedback loop in place, you can begin to experiment in a myriad of ways to see whether subtle changes to your topics, to your tone and style, or to your content have an impact on readership.

The final step is to actively test your hypothesis. The easiest way to do this is to conduct an A/B test. An A/B test refers to the practice—common in advertising—of publishing two advertisements for the same product or service but with a subtle difference in order to evaluate which version of the advertisement has the greatest impact. While the concept may seem foreign in the context of legal publications, it can be easily applied and very effective. If you are experimenting with two formulas for writing an article (see Rule 1: Efficient Writing), or two ways to construct an article's title, consider self-publishing both versions of the same article and then comparing the metrics to determine which variation proved most effective. For example, the following two articles were written on the same topic, published within days of each other, and contain the same substantive information. Each article, however, uses a different style, structure, and approach:

Version	Article A	Article B
Word Count	636 words	996 Words
Title	A €150k Warning—An Update to the GDPR Privacy FAQ: Does a company need to get employees' consent to collect information from them?	A €150k warning to employers—don't ask your employees to consent to your privacy policy!
Text	The European Union's General Data Protection Regulation ("GDPR") is arguably the most comprehensive - and complex - data privacy regulation in the world. Although the GDPR went into force on May 25, 2018, there continues to be a great deal of confusion regarding the requirements of the GDPR. To help address that confusion, Bryan Cave Leighton Paisner published a multi-part series that discussed the questions most frequently asked by clients concerning the GDPR. The following FAQ is updated with the recent decision from the Greek data protection authority to issue an administrative fine for €150k against an employer that sought the consent of its employees to processing. Q: Does a company need to get employees' consent to collect information from them? No.	The Greek data protection authority ("DPA") recently announced a €150,000 fine against a company that required its employees "to provide consent to the processing of their personal data."[1] According to the DPA, as the "[c]onsent of data subjects in the context of employment relations cannot be regarded as freely given due to the clear imbalance between the parties,"[2] by asking for consent the employer had failed to identify the correct legal basis for processing which in turn caused the employer to issue an incorrect privacy notice to its employees (i.e., the privacy notice identified consent as the basis for processing instead of a basis approved by the DPA). While the amount of the fine fell well below the 4% of annual turnover maximum penalty theoretically permitted under the GDPR, its size has sent shockwaves through the human resource community as it represents one of the largest fines issued in the context of employment data. The overall message

Version	Article A	Article B
	While the GDPR recognizes consent as one of the six foundations upon which a company can process information, most European Union Member States are skeptical about whether an employee's consent can be effective given the imbalance of power in the employment relationship. Put differently, many European Union Member States would question whether a consent obtained by an employer was freely given and, therefore, effective. As the Article 29 Working Party—an independent advisory body to the European Commission on data protection matters—has stated:	from the DPA was unmistakable—employers should stop asking their employees to broadly consent to a company's privacy practices.
		While technically the DPA's holding only applies to data that is subject to Greek labor and employment laws, the DPA's viewpoint is likely consistent with that of many supervisory authorities in the other Member States. In terms of understanding the larger context, the GDPR states that a company may process personal data so long as one (or more) of the following six situations applies:[3]
	An imbalance of power … occurs in the employment context. Given the dependency that results from the employer/employee relationship, it is unlikely that the data subject is able to deny his/her employer consent to data processing without experiencing the fear or real risk of detrimental effects as a result of a refusal. It is unlikely that an employee would be able to respond freely to a request for consent from his/her employer to, for example, activate monitoring systems such as camera-observation in a workplace, or to fill out assessment forms, without feeling	1. A data subject has provided consent; 2. The processing is necessary to perform a contract; 3. The processing is necessary to comply with a legal obligation; 4. The processing is necessary to protect the vital interests of a person; 5. The processing is necessary for the performance of a task carried out in the public interest; or 6. The processing is necessary for a legitimate interest pursued by a controller (e.g., an employer) or a third party.

Version	Article A	Article B
	any pressure to consent. Therefore, [the Article 29 Working Party] deems it problematic for employers to process personal data of current or future employees on the basis of consent as it is unlikely to be freely given. For the majority of such data processing at work, the lawful basis cannot and should not be the consent of the employees (Article 6(1a)) due to the nature of the relationship between employer and employee.[1]	Most European Union Member States have been skeptical about whether an employee's consent can be effective given the imbalance of power in the employment relationship. Put differently, many European Union Member States question whether a consent obtained by an employer is freely given and, therefore, effective. The Article 29 Working Party—an independent advisory body to the European Commission on data protection matters that predated the European Data Protection Board—further explained:
	The net result is that under the GDPR, not only is a company not required to obtain the consent of their employees to data processing, in many situations, a company is not permitted to base processing upon consent.	An imbalance of power … occurs in the employment context. Given the dependency that results from the employer/employee relationship, it is unlikely that the data subject is able to deny his/her employer consent to data processing without experiencing the fear or real risk of detrimental effects as a result of a refusal. It is unlikely that an employee would be able to respond freely to a request for consent from his/her employer to, for example, activate monitoring systems such as camera-observation in a workplace, or to fill out assessment forms, without feeling any pressure to consent. Therefore, [the Article 29 Working Party] deems it problematic for
	Some supervisory authorities have brought enforcement actions against companies that have attempted to obtain the consent of employees to process data.[2] For example in July of 2019, the Greek supervisory authority issued a €150,000 administrative fine against a company that required its employees "to provide consent to the processing of their personal data," as the "[c]onsent of data	

Version	Article A	Article B
	subjects in the context of employment relations cannot be regarded as freely given due to the clear imbalance between the parties."[3] The supervisory authority made clear that in its opinion the processing of employment data should be based upon either the performance of the employment contract (i.e., Article 6(1)(b)), the needs of the employer to comply with a legal obligation to process data (i.e., Article 6(1)(c)), or the legitimate interest of the employer to the "smooth and effective operation of the company" (i.e., Article 6(1)(f)).[4]	employers to process personal data of current or future employees on the basis of consent as it is unlikely to be freely given. For the majority of such data processing at work, the lawful basis cannot and should not be the consent of the employees (Article 6(1a)) due to the nature of the relationship between employer and employee.[4] The net result is that under the GDPR in the "majority" of employment situations a company may not be permitted to base processing upon consent. Instead the Greek DPA suggested that most human resource data processing should be based on either the performance of the employment contract, compliance with a legal obligation to which the employer is subject, or the legitimate interest of the employer. It should be noted that the DPA stopped short of saying that no employment-related processing could be based upon consent. While consent is viewed skeptically in the employment context, it is not ineffective in every situation. Consent may be effective and used as a basis for processing where an employer can show that there is relatively

Version	Article A	Article B
		little imbalance of power between the employer and the employee, or if a reasonable employee would understand that there would be no adverse impact if consent were withheld. For example, there would be a strong argument that consent would be effective in the following situations: • Consent obtained from a CEO, or from other senior executives, may be effective as there may be far less of an "imbalance of power" between a senior executive and a company. However another legal basis, rather than consent, should be relied upon if possible. • Consent obtained from employees for the collection of mundane information such as their food preferences (e.g., vegan, vegetarian, etc.) would be effective as an employee is unlikely to believe that they would be at risk of reprisal if they decided not to offer such a preference. • Consent obtained from employees for the collection of information relating to a social activity (e.g., collecting an employee's name in order to be entered into an office raffle) would be effective as an employee is unlikely to believe that they would be at risk of reprisal if they decided not to participate in the activity.

Version	Article A	Article B
		In response to the DPA enforcement, human resource managers should consider taking the following actions: 1. Review your data inventory or record of processing and verify that most Human Resource data is not being processed based upon consent. 2. Review your privacy notice to verify that it does not state or imply that consent is the primary basis upon which data is processed. 3. Review any forms or documents provided to employees for signature to verify that they do not state or imply that personal data is processed based upon consent.
	1. Article 29 Working Party, WP 259: Guidelines on Consent under Regulation 2016/679 at 8 (Nov. 28, 2017) (emphasis added). 2. Summary of Hellenic DPA's Decision No. 26/2019, available at https://www.dpa.gr/pls/portal/docs/PAGE/APDPX/ENGLISH_INDEX/DECISIONS/SUMMARY%20OF%20DECISION%2026_2019%20(EN).PDF (stating that employees were asked to "sign a statement according to which they acknowledged that their personal data kept and processed by the company was directly related to the needs of the employment relationship...."). 3. Id. 4. Id.	1. Summary of Hellenic DPA's Decision No. 26/2019, available at https://www.dpa.gr/pls/portal/docs/PAGE/APDPX/ENGLISH_INDEX/DECISIONS/SUMMARY%20OF%20DECISION%2026_2019%20(EN).PDF. 2. Id. 3. GDPR art. 6(1)(a)–(f). 4. Article 29 Working Party, WP 259: Guidelines on Consent under Regulation 2016/679 at 8 (Nov. 28, 2017).

Among Lexology readers, the articles led to the following readership patterns after one week:

	Article A	Article B
Total Reads	392	590
Percentage In-House	52% (205 of 392)	70% (415 of 590)
Percentage Law Firm	8% (34 of 392)	13% (82 of 590)
Number of Prints	20 prints	20 prints

The differences shown in the above table are significant. Part of the feedback loop, however, is deciphering whether the differences should lead to changes in future article structure (see Rule 1: Efficient Writing). For example, the difference might suggest that the same content has two different potential audiences and, hence, is worth repurposing (see Rule 5: Recycling and the Rule of Threes) for repetition (see Rule 7: Repetition and Stockpiling). While the data is probative, it is important to be cautious in making any permanent changes based upon one data point and to take time to consider what factors may be impacting readership. For example, in a true A/B test, only one variable between the two articles would have been altered (e.g., the title) so any differences in readership could be assumed to be attributable to the change. In the above test, multiple variables were altered—title, length, structure, tone, and style. While one could (and should) speculate about which factor(s) contributed to the divergence in readership, the best use of the statistics is to come up with a hypothesis about what may have had the greatest impact on the readership (e.g., the title) and to test the hypothesis in the next article to be published (i.e., conduct an A/B test of another article on a different topic, but where the title of one version follows the title convention used in Article A above and the title of the other version follows the title convention used in Article B above). The goal here, of course, is not to create two versions of every article that you write or to continually publish the same content. A/B testing should be carried out strategically in order to test a specific hypothesis, not as a system in and of itself for your long-term publishing. If you achieve consistent results across multiple tests, it is a good indication that you should adjust your formula across articles to maximize readership (see Rule 1: Efficient Writing).

In addition to using metrics as a feedback loop, metrics can also be leveraged in their own right for marketing purposes. Specifically, most of the legal publication aggregation services rank those attorneys who are most looked to by companies for information on specific legal topics. Each service differs in the type of rankings that it publishes. For example, some rankings are based simply off of the number of times that an author's publications are viewed; other rankings attempt to gauge user interaction (e.g., how many readers forwarded or shared an article).

To the extent that one of your goals is to be ranked within your area of expertise, there are simple stylistic changes that may impact your score in certain ranking systems. The following describe the five most common factors:

1. *Links to external sources.* User interactions are often monitored and tracked by aggregation services and form one of the metrics used to rank authors. While there may be many types of user interactions that are monitored (e.g., how long a user spends reading your article, whether the user completes your article, whether a user prints your article, or whether a user forwards your article), one form of user interaction that is often tracked is whether a user clicks a link within your article. Encouraging users to click links is one of the easiest ways to boost your user interaction. There are ways to generate user interaction through hyperlinks that provide a more useful resource to your readers. The easiest is simply to add a link to the primary text of any statutes, regulations, or cases that you cite in an article.

2. *Links to your other articles.* When deciding which attorneys are the most looked-to resources on a certain topic, one of the factors that aggregation services look at is the total number of "reads" of your body of work during a given time period. One way to increase your overall number

of reads is to include hyperlinks to previous articles that you published on related topics. This might be as simple as dropping a footnote that references a prior article or hyperlinking statutory citations or cases that you discuss at greater length in other publications. If a reader views your first article and opens two links to your previous works, the aggregation service will not only count the links as "interactions" (see previous item) but will likely count three "views" of your articles instead of one.

3. *Primary keywords.* Most aggregation services function by collecting website publications across law firms and then scanning the content for keywords that indicate that an article relates to a certain topic (e.g., Labor and Employment, Export Controls, or Leases). Articles are categorized based on those keywords and are distributed to individuals (e.g., in-house counsel) who sign up to receive information on a specific topic. For example, if you published an article on the Fair Credit Reporting Act, an aggregation service might identify the word "FCRA" within your article and then distribute the article to attorneys who have signed up for updates relating to the FCRA. In order to optimize the distribution of your articles, remember to include keywords that a search engine would likely recognize to correctly classify your article. For example, if your article deals with background checks (which are regulated by the FCRA), make sure to include the word "FCRA" somewhere in the text so that the article gets correctly indexed. If instead your article refers obliquely to "federal and state laws governing background checks," there is a chance that it would fail to be correctly indexed as dealing with the FCRA.

4. *Secondary keywords.* As discussed in the previous item, aggregation services utilize keyword searches to categorize articles for distribution to specific lists. It is often worth registering as a reader with an aggregation service to see what distribution lists they offer. If you know the categories that the service is trying to identify, you can

consciously include secondary keywords that are likely to cause the aggregation service to index your article in multiple categories (and hence distribute your article to multiple groups of potential readers). In the context of the preceding example, if you are aware that the aggregation service maintains lists for "labor and employment," "employee discrimination," "human resources management," and "FCRA," you might include within the text of your article additional keywords that would ensure that the article gets picked up in all four lists. For example, the following paragraph would likely trigger all of the lists:

> **Human resources managers** often struggle with how to conduct background checks consistent with the **Fair Credit Reporting Act** ("**FCRA**"). One of their main concerns is that, from a **labor and employment** perspective, their use of background checks does not create an environment ripe for allegations of **employee discrimination**.

5. *Titles*. Finally, no factor has a greater impact on whether someone reads an article than its title. If a title is too obscure, a reader may have no idea that the article discusses something of relevance. For example, a recent article was published with the title "A Delicate Balance." While the article might attract some readers based purely upon curiosity, the readers whom it draws are not likely to be engaged in the content. Put differently, nobody would know from the title that the article actually dealt with export control sanctions, and it would be pure coincidence if anyone who opened the article out of curiosity had an interest in export control sanctions. While authors fear titles that are "boring," titles that are descriptive (even to the point of being boring) ensure that an article finds the right audience. A final word about titles. If you remember reading, or writing, journal articles in law school, you may recall that many law school professors make a point of coming up with creative legal puns in

their titles. Indeed, some spend immense amounts of time elevating the cryptic nature of titles to a form of esoteric art. For example, while drafting this chapter, I opened up the Harvard Law Review and saw the following title of one of the articles: *Neo-?*[2] Or consider the following from the law review of my alma mater:

> *The Miseducation of Free Speech*[3]
> *The Great Unfulfilled Promise of* Tinker[4]

Because we all were exposed to the same academic training, the first instinct of many practicing attorneys when they draft an article is to copy this style of article title selection. It's important to remember that the audience of a professor writing for a law review is very different from the audience of practicing attorneys. Law review articles are typically written for a small group of legal experts who are intensely focused on a single issue and in some cases are used to having public discourse via article writing. They are also explicitly, or implicitly, trying to convince others (i.e., readers, tenure committees, or their colleagues at other schools) of their intellectual prowess. How better to do that than to create a riddle in an article title that is either intended to make the reader expend energy to decipher its meaning or intended to convey to readers that only someone with the author's level of intelligence would truly understand the meaning? Your audience—in-house counsel and business clients—is very different. They don't want to expend energy to understand what you are writing about, nor do they want to engage in, or be the bystanders of, an academic publication discourse. They are looking for short

---

2. Adrian Vermeule, *Neo-?*, 133 HARV. L. REV. F. 103 (Mar. 2, 2020) (responding to Jeffrey A. Pojanowski, *Neoclassical Administrative Law*).

3. Mary Anne Franks, *The Miseducation of Free Speech*, 105 VA. L. REV. ONLINE 218 (2019).

4. Mary-Rose Papandrea, *The Great Unfulfilled Promise of* Tinker, 105 VA. L. REV. ONLINE 159 (2019).

(see Rule 2: Short) and business-practical (see Rule 3: Business Practical) information—not a brain teaser.

With any ranking system comes the ability to game or manipulate the rankings. While the following practices may push up the rankings of an article, I strongly recommend that you *stay clear* as they jeopardize credibility and, in so doing, undercut efforts to establish a persona of expertise:

1. *Clickbait*. We all have seen examples of clickbait in our daily news feeds—i.e., articles whose title is controversial or shocking and is designed for the sole purpose of encouraging people to click. While most attorneys steer clear of clickbait, it still exists. Take for example the following article that was written about a European data privacy regulation that had been anticipated for several years: "New EU ePrivacy Regulation to Come into Force in 2019: What to Expect." The EU ePrivacy Regulation was a closely watched and long-anticipated rule among data privacy attorneys, and the title of the article implied that the regulation was finally coming into force. Almost every data privacy attorney in the world (or at least in Europe and in the United States) clicked on the article to read the long-awaited announcement. In actuality, the article did not discuss when (or if) the ePrivacy Regulation would come into force in 2019, other than to state in passing that it "should be adopted sometime in early 2019" (it did not in fact get enacted or go into force in 2019). Even though the authors generated a large quantity of page hits, I do *not* recommend engaging in clickbait. The readers who visited the above article either viewed the authors as not knowing what they were talking about or were annoyed that they had been tricked into giving up their limited time to read an article that was not of high value.

2. *Pagination*. Another trick we have all seen in general media is the use of pagination. This describes the practice of breaking an article into several webpages in order to force a reader to continue to click through to read the whole article, thus generating additional links and page

views. For aggregation services that score "interactions," those links to additional pages may boost an author's rankings. So, for example, if you click on an article titled "The Top Ten Best Beach Resorts," you might find yourself clicking "next" as you read through each item of the top ten list. The publisher structured the article in this manner to count ten page views for every person who tried to read the article and to provide ten times the number of banner ads to each reader. While pagination has the ability to push up page views and content interaction, which, as discussed above, may increase standing on certain aggregation services, the use of pagination interrupts the flow of articles and is annoying to many readers. In other words, *do not* use pagination to boost your author statistics.

RULE 6: FREQUENTLY ASKED QUESTIONS

Question 1: Do Bigger Metrics Always Mean That an Article Is Better When It Comes to Business Development?

No. As discussed earlier, there are techniques that can push up an article's readership but do so in a manner that does not accomplish your goal of conveying expertise to readers. Clickbait and pagination are two examples of counterproductive strategies.

Even if you are not trying to manipulate readership, there are situations in which the number of readers does not necessarily correlate to the effectiveness of your article at business development. For example, if your area of law is extremely narrow and your potential clients are comprised of a small clique of specialized attorneys, relatively small readership might be expected and a small overall readership count could still be a success in terms of promoting your brand recognition. It's for this reason that you should try to establish your own baseline when it comes to article readership—i.e., what is the average read of articles that are written in your industry or written by you concerning a particular topic? Establishing your own baseline and then using it to gauge whether a particular article is more or less effective than your average article can be more effective than comparing your readership numbers to another attorney whose target audience may be bigger.

Question 2: Does It Matter Which Analytics Service You Use to Get Metrics?

Yes and no.

As I suggest in this chapter, there are pros and cons to each source of analytics. Almost all analytics services report on the quantity of people who read articles on their platform, whether that platform is a general-purpose social media platform (e.g., LinkedIn) or a service for republishing law firm articles (e.g., Lexology). As a result, the metrics that a particular analytics service reports have just as much to do with the type of individuals who subscribe to their service or use their platform as the number of people who want to read your article. The net result is that if your intended audience is comprised of chief financial officers or chief operating officers, they might be unlikely to view your article on a service that republishes and aggregates legal articles for in-house counsel. A low readership on a service like Lexology or JD Supra might not indicate that your article did not reach its intended audience. From that perspective, it does matter which analytics service you use to get metrics, and ideally you would choose an analytics service that accurately samples the audience that you intend to reach.

On the other hand, there is no perfect source of analytics. Put differently, it's simply not possible to track each and every person who reads your article in the various formats and places that it may find itself. That is not in and of itself a problem, as the goal when looking at metrics is not to capture complete information about the absolute impact that your article has (i.e., how many people actually read it) but to capture accurate information about the relative impact that your article has (i.e., was your last article more or less effective than your articles on average?).

I recommend identifying all the sources for metrics that track readership among what you believe is your target audience and among those sources identifying the source that is the easiest for you to use and to check. The most important thing is that you find a way to integrate metrics into your writing routine—not that you necessarily find the holy grail for the most reliable metrics.

Question 3: Do All Analytics Services Count "Reads" in the Same Way?

No. While most of the analytics services are cryptic concerning how they track readership, there appear to be differences concerning how they compute the number of times that an article is read. For example, some analytics services try to deduplicate reads and identify only the number of unique individuals who have read your article. In other words, if one person opens your article two or three times a day (or hits the refresh button a dozen times), the service counts it as "one" read. Other analytics services try to account for instances in which your article is accessed but may not be read. For example, "bots" and webcrawlers routinely search the Internet for content. Some services have systems in place to ensure that when these computer programs open your article and "read" it, those reads are not reported to you as reads by actual people.

Question 4: Are All Analytics Services Free?

No. Some analytics services are free. For example, most of the free online social media platforms provide some level of analytics to authors at no charge. Other analytics require a subscription or a paid enrollment.

Question 5: If an Analytics Service Reports on Several Types of Metrics, Which Metric Should I Pay the Most Attention To?

I find that the most important single statistic you can look at on a routine basis is the number of views (or if available the number of unique views) of your article. That said, if your analytics service provides more granular information, that can be useful to do a deeper dive concerning the impact that your article writing may have. For example, some analytics services provide the following types of information:

Titles of your readers. If available, this information can be useful to better understand whether your articles are reaching the right level of seniority within a company. For example, if the type of decision maker who typically would retain you is a general counsel (as opposed to an associate general counsel, senior counsel, or deputy general counsel), knowing the percentage of your readers who hold the title of general counsel is important for your own feedback loop.

Types of organizations. If available, knowing whether your readers are from outside law firms, companies, governments, or nonprofits can be useful to better understand whether your articles are, again, reaching their intended audience. If you are an outside counsel whose target audience is corporate in-house counsel, if you find that the majority of your readers are from other law firms (i.e., your competitors), that may signal that you need to adapt your article topics to address what your target audience cares most about (see Rule 3: Business Practical).

Interactions. While this chapter discusses user interactions in the context of their impact on rankings, measuring user interactions can independently be a source of information in terms of better targeting your publications. For example, if readers printed or downloaded one of your articles at an unusually high rate, it may signal that they found the content particularly interesting and important and, therefore, wanted to ensure that they had access to the information at a later time. Similarly, if users forwarded one of your articles at an unusually high rate, it may signal that they believe the content would be of interest to their colleagues or other people in their industry.

Question 6: How Long Should I Wait before Looking at the Metrics of an Article?

As discussed in this chapter, in order for a feedback loop to be effective, it's important to get feedback close in time to when you published an article. That said, for metrics to be accurate, you have to wait at least some amount of time to get an accurate reading on an article's effectiveness. I find that three days typically strikes the right balance of ensuring that enough time has elapsed to gather data but not too much time has elapsed to make the data meaningless or distant.

Question 7: Does the Electronic Format in Which I Publish (e.g., PDF or HTML) Impact Metrics?

It can. If you publish in PDF, make sure that your PDF files are searchable (i.e., that the text within the PDF can be scanned and read online). If the PDF file is not searchable, then potential readers may not be able to find your article when they use search engines. In addition, aggregation services may not be able to find your articles, republish them, appropriately index them, or serve them to the right interest groups. Even if your articles are searchable, if the PDFs are heavily formatted, aggregation services may require users who click on the title of your article to click once, or twice, more to download the PDF. In other words, if an aggregation service cannot automatically scrape the content of your article and re-serve it on their platform, they may need to send potential readers back to the original online document. Requiring a potential reader to click more than once or twice may discourage them from investing the time to read your article. As a result, I typically recommend publishing articles in HTML unless there is a specific need or benefit to publishing in PDF (e.g., charts, tables, or graphics that will not display correctly in HTML).

Rule 6: Reminders

Do	Don't Do
✓ Investigate what metrics are collected by the sources that publish, or republish, your articles.	✗ Publish articles without checking your own metrics.
✓ Familiarize yourself with the level of detail offered by the available metrics.	✗ Continue to publish articles on a topic that continually receives low readership.
✓ Choose one source of metrics to check against all of your articles.	✗ Continue to publish articles using a format that continually receives low readership.
✓ Review your readership metrics several times per week and shortly after you publish each article.	✗ Use titles that are designed to generate clicks but, when an article is read, do not convey that you have topical expertise.
✓ Identify which of your articles performed better or worse in terms of readership.	✗ Break a single article into several pieces that a reader must click through for the purpose of generating clicks.
✓ Look for trends in terms of what might be responsible for higher readership rates.	✗ Use vague or ambiguous titles.
✓ Test your hypothesis by conducting your own A/B test.	
✓ Integrate information that you deduce from your metrics into future article writing.	
✓ Include links to external sources (e.g., primary sources) in your articles.	
✓ Include links to your other publications in your articles.	
✓ Include keywords that might help readers (or search engines) identify your article as relating to a certain topic.	
✓ Include keywords that might help identify your article as relevant to several groups of readers.	
✓ Use titles that describe what the article is actually about.	

Rule 6: Worksheet

1. Investigate what metrics are available for the articles that you published and write down the source of the metrics here: Metrics Source 1: _____ Metrics Source 2: _____ Metrics Source 3: _____
2. For each metrics source, look at what type of information is available and might be useful for future tracking. Pick one source to "follow" going forward.
3. Pull the data available from that source for all of the articles that you have published.
4. Identify the most and least popular articles. Does the popularity correlate to what you expected?
5. What is the average readership for the articles that you published over the last year? What was your highest readership? Average Readership: _____ Highest Readership: _____
6. Identify any trends among the articles that performed the best. Do those trends suggest a topic, style, or structure that you should consider replicating going forward?
7. Identify any trends among the articles that performed the worst. Do those trends suggest a topic, style, or structure to avoid going forward?
8. Based upon your metrics, try to identify the topic, style, and structure of a future article that you believe is most likely to have the highest readership. Write the title here. Title: _____
9. Draft the article and check its metrics. Did it perform as expected? Did it beat your average? How did it compare to your most popular article?
10. For each new article that you publish, think about how to beat your average (at a minimum) and how you might beat your highest readership.

CHAPTER 11

Rule 7: Repetition and Stockpiling

Repetition makes reputation.

—Elizabeth Arden

As I discussed in Chapter 2, writing one article (or even three articles) does not in and of itself constitute expertise-driven marketing.

To provide perspective, in any given year I will write between one hundred and two hundred articles. Of course, every article is not completely unique or different. Following Rule 1 (Efficient Writing), most of my articles have similar structures and formats and contain shared features or introductions. Following Rule 5 (Recycling and the Rule of Threes), many of my articles will also contain material that is partially repurposed from other articles. Still, there are no two ways about it—two hundred articles is a lot and takes a significant investment of time.

You may be asking whether it is really necessary to publish that many articles. It's a fair question. In truth, there is no magic number of articles that you need to publish to sell your expertise, but there is rhyme and reason to publishing a large quantity of articles.

When I was a young attorney, and before I could claim to be associated with any area of expertise, I remember going to a dinner party with my wife, who was doing a fellowship at a hospital. The host of the party was a well-known and much-cited doctor. I recall asking him how he became so recognized. He explained that he had published a dozen articles on the same (somewhat esoteric) ethical dilemma. I asked him whether he intended to publish any additional articles and, if so, on what topic. His answer was simple—he was working on another article on the same somewhat esoteric ethical dilemma. I asked him how he decided to focus on that topic, and his answer (and his explanation) has stuck with me ever since.

He said that he could have written a dozen articles on a dozen different topics, but, if he had done so, he probably would not be recognized for anything. Instead, he wrote over a dozen articles on the same topic—more than anyone else in his field— which meant that *nobody* could write on the same issue without citing him (usually repeatedly) and discussing his body of work. In other words, the quantity of his writing—just as much as the uniqueness of his ideas—made him the topic expert.

There was another benefit of writing on the same topic. Each of his articles contained about 90 percent shared content. For example, each article set up the history of the topic, described the dilemma, and described the previous work done on the topic. The last 10 percent of each article discussed a new aspect of the dilemma—either a new perspective, new research, or a new application of the underlying principles. In essence, he had found a way to recycle (Rule 5: Recycling and the Rule of Threes) and to use a formulaic style (Rule 1: Efficient Writing), thus lowering the effort that was required for each article but, at the same time, optimizing his name and expertise recognition. Simply brilliant.

He did not, of course, invent the concept of repetition. Many attorneys intuitively know it and apply it in their substantive practice. For example, when I was a young attorney and went through an advanced trial advocacy program, the seasoned litigator who led the program ordered us—in a manner reminiscent of a drill sergeant—to always remember recency and repetition. What she meant was that a litigator should repeat, as often as possible and at every turn, the theme that they wanted the jury to remember. No matter how much you felt internally like a broken record, she emphasized that the jury needed to hear that theme—that theory of the case—over and over during the opening, the cross-examinations, the direct examinations, and, ultimately, the closing. While it felt repetitive, ultimately, she was right. Repetition works.

So how do you apply the concept of repetition in article writing, and how do you increase your current quantity of writing?

There are several techniques for increasing the quantity of your writing and thus increasing the repetitiveness with which clients and potential clients see your name.

First, don't get intimidated by big numbers. A decade ago, I was probably publishing five to ten articles a year. If, at the time, I had said to myself that I was going to publish two hundred articles a year (a 2,000 percent increase), I would have been paralyzed by the enormity of the proposition.

Second, repetition is about quantity, but it is also about consistent frequency. Instead of setting an absolute number as your end goal, think in terms of a manageable cadence. For example, what if you sat down over a weekend and wrote 12 one-page articles? If you spaced out the release of those articles, you could publish an article once a month, every month, for a year. Start there. Sit down and write 12 articles. Once you are done, stockpile them—i.e., don't publish them all at once. Instead, take out a calendar and schedule them to be published on the first Monday of each month. Because your articles are shelf stable (Rule 4), there is no urgency to get them out. They will be just as relevant when they are published in a month or two as they are today. By spacing them out, you have guaranteed that your clients, or potential clients, will see your name in their inbox repeatedly throughout the year (i.e., a minimum of once a month). In other words, you will have met Rule 7 by publishing at a minimum level of repetition.

Third, try to increase your article cadence in the short term—*not* the long term. What does that mean? Your 12 articles guarantee you a once-a-month backbone for your publishing year. Now, if you thought about going to a biweekly schedule for the year, you might shudder at the idea of drafting another 12 articles right away. If you thought about going to a weekly schedule for the entire year, drafting an additional 40 articles would probably feel impossible. Instead, think about the short term. On a calendar, write down the names of the publications that you intend to send out the first Monday of every month (you can find a blank monthly calendar in Appendix C). Now, on the third Monday of every month, write "Possible Extra Article" as a placeholder:

MONDAY	TUESDAY	WEDNESDAY	THURSDAY	FRIDAY
1 PREWRITTEN ARTICLE TITLE: #####	2	3	4	5
8	9	10	11	12
15 Possible Extra Article	16	17	18	19
22	23	24	25	26
29	30	31	1	2

Focus only on the month at hand and see if writing one more article is a realistic time commitment and an achievable goal. If you do it, just for the current month, you would have temporarily moved to a biweekly publication schedule.

Fourth, play it by ear to see what you feel like writing after that. If you followed Rule 1 and have created an efficient writing structure and Rule 2 and have made your articles short, you may find yourself coming up with other article ideas throughout the month. If that happens, instead of immediately publishing the new articles that you write, add them to the next available "Possible Extra Article" biweekly slot in your calendar. In other words, begin to stockpile them so that your *temporary* biweekly publication schedule becomes a permanent biweekly publication schedule.

Fifth, if your stockpile starts to get big, increase your cadence. Besides my core backbone of articles, which might span the year to guarantee that I have a monthly article, I try not to keep a stockpile of more than three months. Therefore, if you find that you have taken up all your "Possible Extra Article" days for the upcoming three months, open up a new "Possible Extra Article" day (e.g., the second Monday of the month). Start scheduling articles into that second extra Monday of the month slot until, again, your stockpile spans three months.

To summarize, the first 12 articles are a commitment to publish and a guarantee that you will have repetition throughout the year that will ensure name awareness and recognition. After that commitment has been made, you don't need to push yourself to commit to other "big chunks" of articles. If you have found a good structure and a good cadence, relatively small quantities of articles (e.g., three articles at a time) will naturally push your cadence from monthly to bimonthly to weekly.

RULE 7: FREQUENTLY ASKED QUESTIONS

Question 1: What Is Your Publication Cadence?

For my particular area of practice, I have found that the most effective cadence is to publish every business day or every other business day. At different points throughout the year, and depending upon the size of my stockpile, I therefore switch from a daily publication cycle to an every-other-day publication cycle.

Question 2: Is Daily Publication Too Much?

Not necessarily.

Many attorneys worry that if they overpublish, they may annoy clients. I find that if you are publishing high-quality material, overpublishing is not a problem. If you are concerned about it, however, and if you operate a mailing list, you can transmit all of your publications to the list as part of a weekly digest so as not to clutter inboxes with a daily e-mail.

If you operate an e-mail mailing list, a good way to gauge if your publications are too frequent is to periodically check the quantity of "unsubscribe" requests that you receive. If you move to a daily publication schedule and your rate of unsubscribe requests does not increase, it is a good indication that your audience does not view your publication cadence as being too much.

Question 3: How Far Can Your Stockpile Go?

Theoretically there is no limit as to how far your stockpile can stretch. That said, and even if you drafted your articles to be shelf stable (Rule 4), if your stockpile stretches too far into the future, you run the risk that there may be a change in law that makes an article out of date before it is published. Beyond the core group of articles that I might draft for the year, I try to keep a stockpile that is no more than six months and no less than three months.

Question 4: Can You Write Everything for the Year at Once?

It's possible. A number of years ago, my team decided that we would attempt to write the majority of our publications during a single sitting. We marked a day on the calendar around the first of the year and tried to block out our schedules, and everyone on our team sat down and during an eight-hour period tried to draft about 100 articles that followed a similar structure (Rule 1), were short (Rule 2), were business practical (Rule 3), and were shelf stable (Rule 4). During the course of the year, other articles were written as new topics and ideas presented themselves, but on January 1, we functionally had two articles a week planned for every week through the following Christmas.

Question 5: Should You Organize Your Stockpile and Be Strategic about When You Release Each Article?

If you create a stockpile of articles, there is a natural inclination to try to be strategic about the time at which you release each article. Sometimes the strategy might try to tie specific articles to specific events on the calendar (e.g., a labor-and-employment-themed article for Boss's Day); other times the strategy might be to release types of articles on particular days of the week. While there is nothing wrong with trying to be strategic about where and when you release an article from your stockpile, I generally find that the logistics involved with trying to time the release of certain articles from your stockpile can be significant and outweigh the usefulness of a timed release strategy.

Question 6: Does It Matter What Day of the Week You Publish On?

Yes and no.

Anecdotally I've been told that it's best to publish an article Tuesday, Wednesday, or Thursday, because people are too busy on Friday trying to wrap up projects and too busy on Monday trying to get back in the swing of things to read articles. That may be true, but I've found that trying to time the release of an article is difficult, if not impossible, given the multiple sources that may pick up your article and the delay in disseminating information online. For example, if you published an article to your mailing list and on your law firm's website on a Thursday but Google did not index/reindex your firm's website until Friday, then your effort to try to publish in the middle of the week backfires, as the majority of the world can't access or find your article until Friday. Some of the aggregation services also do not scan law firm websites daily, so you may end up publishing an article on your law firm's website on a Friday and it doesn't get scanned and republished until the following Tuesday.

All in all, I've given up any attempt to target a particular day of the week for publication.

Rule 7: Reminders

Do	Don't Do
✓ Create a publication calendar in which you plan when articles are going to be released. ✓ Decide upon an initial cadence of publications (e.g., once a month, twice a month, etc.). ✓ Create a skeleton of shelf-stable publications at the beginning of the year that satisfy that initial cadence. ✓ Build around your core skeleton by drafting additional articles that are then scheduled at regular intervals and stockpiled. ✓ If your stockpile exceeds three months of material, increase the cadence (e.g., go from biweekly to weekly, or from weekly to twice weekly).	✗ Write articles about topics that are not shelf stable, as they can't be scheduled for the future. ✗ Commit to a publication schedule (e.g., monthly) without predrafting the articles that will be scheduled for the entire year. ✗ Commit to a publication schedule (e.g., weekly) that requires predrafting an imposing number of articles.

Rule 7: Worksheet

1. Brainstorm 12 shelf-stable (Rule 4) article topics that will form the skeleton, or backbone, of a monthly publication schedule. Consider making the 12 articles part of a single series or using the same formulaic efficient writing style (see Rule 1: Efficient Writing). Write the topics here:

Topic 1: _____

Topic 2: _____

Topic 3: _____

Topic 4: _____

Topic 5: _____

Topic 6: _____

Topic 7: _____

Topic 8: _____

Topic 9: _____

Topic 10: _____

Topic 11: _____

Topic 12: _____

2. Write the 12 articles listed above, but do not publish any of the articles until all of them are written. In other words, stockpile the articles until all 12 are complete.

3. Once the articles are complete, use the calendar in Appendix C to schedule the articles to be published on the first Monday of each month through the end of the year. You are now a monthly publisher!

4. Write on your calendar for the third Monday of each month "Possible Extra Article." If you write any additional articles, schedule each one into an available "Possible Extra Article" slot. If all of the Possible Extra Article slots are full for the next three months, write on your calendar for the second and/or fourth Monday of each month another "Possible Extra Article" and begin scheduling into those slots. You are now a biweekly publisher!

5. Continue to stockpile articles such that they are being released in an organized cadence that remains consistent for the upcoming three months.

CHAPTER 12

Rule 8: Do It Yourself

If you want a thing done well, do it yourself.

—*Napoleon Bonaparte*

My first experience with legal article writing came as a first-year associate when a partner asked me if I would help write an article for an industry newsletter. My immediate reaction, of course, was "yes."

The article was hard to write. As a first-year associate, I was not familiar with the topic. Let's be honest, I was not familiar with *any* topic. Everything I did was new. I also was uncertain about the correct tone, style, and format. Finally, I didn't know how much I needed to explain to the reader. Were they coming to the topic new to the law like I was? Were they new to the field? Or should I assume that they already knew most of the basics that I was trying to learn? Looking back, I shudder to think about how many hours I probably put into that project. Now that I am a partner, I also shudder to think about what type of work product I ultimately turned in and how much work the partner had to put in to fix or rewrite it.

I waited a few weeks and then the newsletter came out. My article was there, but my name was not on it.

That experience taught me two things.

First, I did not like ghostwriting articles for other people. It's true that I was an associate, and, as an employee, I was getting paid to write. On some level, it should not have mattered to me whether what I wrote was attributed to me, right? Wrong. Whether you are an intern, staff attorney, associate, counsel, or partner, article writing may be part of your job, but at most firms it's not a part of your job for which there is direct remuneration. Put differently, there is always an element of voluntary business development when it comes to article writing, and if you don't receive a byline, then there is not much "business development" taking place (at least not for you).

Second, having me draft the article was horribly inefficient. My lack of substantive knowledge and my lack of experience meant that I invested ten hours for every one hour that it would have taken an experienced attorney to draft the same article. That calculus might still be efficient if, by investing ten hours, I saved the partner from having to do the work. I'm almost certain that was not the case. After I invested ten hours, the partner probably had to spend more time fixing my work than he would have needed to draft the article from scratch.

The pattern of partners and counsel pushing down article writing to junior associates continues to happen across many practice areas. It is also one of the biggest traps in expertise-driven marketing.

Don't misunderstand me—there are many good reasons a partner might want to collaborate with a junior associate on a writing project. Writing projects can be a way to expose an associate to a substantive area in which they might lack expertise. Writing projects can also be a way to help train an associate on how to write or to find an excuse to work with a colleague for the first time. Delegating for one of those reasons may make good sense. If you do that, however, be cognizant that your main goal should be, and is, to train the associate and *not* to engage in expertise-driven marketing. In other words, you should not expect a junior associate who is not already an expert in the subject area, does not have experience in efficient writing (Rule 1), does not have practice drafting short articles (Rule 2), and has little exposure to what are likely to be business-practical solutions (Rule 3) to be your main strategy to create and communicate your expertise. There is simply no replacement for your own time if you intend to pursue an expertise-driven marketing strategy.

The principle of "do it yourself" applies just as well to collaborations with other partners, counsel, or senior associates.

Working with senior attorneys who have expertise that rivals your own does not involve the same types of inefficiencies as delegating to a junior attorney who does not (through no fault of their own) have expertise. It still involves inefficiencies, however. Unless both collaborators are well-seasoned expertise-driven marketers, each attorney typically ends up taking more time to coauthor than one attorney would have spent authoring the entire publication. In addition, neither attorney is forced to fully engage with the project in the way necessary to hone a writing structure (Rule 1: Efficient Writing), streamline text (Rule 2: Short), concentrate on business-actionable solutions (Rule 3: Business Practical), or think about how content might have multiple purposes and incarnations (Rule 5: Recycling and the Rule of Threes).

Just the logistics of coauthoring can erode efficiencies between experienced attorneys. Later in my career, I was asked to edit a chapter of a treatise for the American Bar Association. The pitch was that it would be relatively little work, as I would have a team of five volunteers from various law firms who would write the individual sections of the chapter. As the editor, all I would need to do was coordinate the efforts of the writers, review the final work product, identify any errors or issues, and standardize the text. My life became a scheduling nightmare as I had to coordinate the schedules of five attorneys, push deadlines (and reminders of deadlines) to each, review and re-review work product, provide feedback and commentary to each of the authors, and then, again, push deadlines (and reminders of deadlines) for final work product. At some point I realized that I had invested more time in the logistics and review process than would have been needed if I just sat down and wrote the entire chapter myself. I also realized that my return on investment was less through the coordination exercise than it would have been had I been the sole author. It was the worst of all worlds—I invested more time, doing activities that I found less rewarding, and had to share the credit among a group of people.

RULE 8: FREQUENTLY ASKED QUESTIONS

Question 1: Do You Ever Coauthor Articles?

Yes.

The purpose of Rule 8 is not to say that you should never coauthor publications; there are good reasons to do so. The purpose of Rule 8 is to make clear that business development through article writing is not something that you can outsource. If you intend to write the quantity and quality of articles needed to sell yourself as having best-in-class expertise, then you need to be willing to invest a significant quantity of your own time in the writing process. The majority of that time will likely be writing articles yourself as the only author, but some of that time may include contributing to joint writing projects.

Question 2: What Percentage of Your Articles Do You Coauthor?

In the year preceding the publication of this book, I solo-authored 158 articles and coauthored 26 articles. In other words, 85 percent of my writing projects involved me as the only author, and 15 percent of my writing projects were collaborations. While the quantity of articles that I write in a given year changes, the ratio of self-written to collaborative projects is relatively consistent.

Question 3: Do You Ever Sign Your Name to an Article Written by an Associate?

I try *never* to ask another attorney to ghostwrite an article for me. As discussed earlier, I do not like to ghostwrite articles for other people and suspect that other people do not like to ghostwrite articles for me.

Question 4: When You Coauthor, How Much Time and Effort Does Each Author Contribute?

I don't think that there is a hard-and-fast rule concerning how much time each author must contribute, and on most projects it is not as simple as each author contributing exactly 50 percent to the writing effort. My personal rule is that if I contribute at least 25 percent of the content of an article (e.g., one in four words), then I seek byline attribution. If I contribute less than 25 percent of the content of an article, I rarely ask for my name to be included as an author and, instead, view my role as more advisory or supervisory. Conversely, when others contribute to an article that I have written, I try to apply the same rule. If someone has contributed at least 25 percent of the article, I list them as a coauthor; if less than 25 percent, I might not.

Question 5: Is It Efficient to Have a Partner Write Articles Instead of Bill Time?

Yes.

There is a perception among some partners that writing articles is something that should be pushed down to associates as the partner spends their time focused on client and billable matters. I take the opposite view.

If you compare expertise-driven marketing to relationship-driven marketing, no partner would ever take the position that having lunch with a client is not an efficient use of their time and they should send an associate instead while they focus on a billable matter. Quite the contrary, most partners would realize that touching base with their clients is the best use of their time in order to generate the billable work that will keep others on their team busy. The same is true for expertise-driven marketing. As discussed earlier, when it comes to writing content that is business practical (Rule 3), strategic, and efficient (Rule 1), partners have a distinct comparative advantage. What might take a partner one hour to draft might take a junior associate five or six hours, and, in some cases, a junior associate may simply lack the knowledge, experience, or skill set to provide business-practical advice. The net result is that if a partner's business development strategy is focused on expertise-driven marketing, the partner has to invest the personal time to write the articles to generate business.

Question 6: Do You Believe That a Junior Associate Should Never Write Articles?

Junior associates, midlevel associates, and senior associates can all be engaged in article writing. It is sometimes harder for junior associates to create articles efficiently, however, as some junior associates must invest time to learn at the same time as they are writing and may lack the business-related experience to provide business-practical information.

Question 7: Doesn't Having Associates Write Articles Train Them?

Yes and no.

Writing articles can train associates on how to write articles. As a result, if an associate is interested in expertise-driven marketing, by all means a partner or supervisor should encourage them to write.

If the goal is to train an associate about a substantive area of law, or to hone the associate's legal writing, and the article is thought of as merely the vehicle to provide that training, it may be less effective. Because effective articles are short (Rule 2) and focused on the business-practical aspects of a topic (Rule 3), they do not necessarily provide an associate who is unfamiliar with an area of law the opportunity to develop a baseline level of knowledge about a topic. In addition, because effective articles are designed to be formulaic and efficient (Rule 1), they may not involve the same style, tone, and structure as traditional legal writing. As a result, if the goal is to help an associate hone their formal legal writing skills, it may not be the best vehicle.

Question 8: If You Are a Partner, How Can You Help Train and Support Your Associates in Their Own Article Writing?

I firmly believe that partners should encourage and foster an associate's interest in business development through expertise-driven marketing. There are a number of easy ways to do so.

First, consider teaching them the rules discussed in this book.

Second, realize that some rules may be more difficult for the associate to address on their own, depending upon their experience level. In particular, it is sometimes difficult for associates to discern what information is business practical versus practical only for lawyers. Depending on whether an associate has worked inside of a company before, it may be difficult for a more junior associate to understand what is realistic when it comes to actions that an in-house counsel can take. Making yourself available to discuss with an associate what is, and what is not, a business-practical interpretation of a particular issue can be invaluable.

Third, if your law firm requires that associates' articles be approved by a partner prior to publication, make yourself available to quickly review and approve publications. There is nothing more discouraging to an associate than to invest significant nonbillable time to write an article and then watch the article go into the black hole of a partner's inbox waiting for approval.

Fourth, make clear to your associates that if they invest the time in writing an article, they will receive byline credit. As discussed above, associates who believe that they will receive no public recognition for an article will not view article writing as an effective means for them to develop, or market, their own expertise.

Question 9: Can an Associate Say No If a Partner Asks Them to Ghostwrite an Article?

In large law firm environments, it's difficult to say no if a partner asks you to write an article, just as it is difficult to object if you write an article for a partner and then they remove your name and add their own. While I try never to take credit for the work of the associates who work for me and similarly counsel my partners against disincentivizing associates by asking them (or expecting them) to ghostwrite articles, unfortunately the practice still happens at firms across the country. So, if you are an associate, what can you do in order to avoid the ghostwriting problem?

Well, it's not as easy or as simple as just saying no. A no can be incorrectly perceived by a partner as indicating that you are not a team player, you do not care about marketing, or you do not care about supporting the larger practice.

When I was a junior associate, I brought this problem to one of my partner mentors, and he imparted some very wise (and practical) advice on how to say no in a way that did not attach to it any stigma. He told me that I should always have two of my own article-writing projects "on deck" at any point in time. He then said that the next time that a partner who I knew was likely to take credit (and give me none) asked me to write an article for them, I should very tactfully say, "I would love to collaborate on a project, but, unfortunately, I am already in the process of writing two articles and want to make sure that I do not overcommit my time." If a partner is not committed to truly wanting to *collaborate* on an article and is instead looking for an associate to push an article-writing obligation onto, nine times out of ten, they will move on to another associate who is not already engaged in business development or article writing. In other words, the best way to avoid the ghostwriting problem is to follow Rule 8 and do it yourself!

Rule 8: Reminders

Do	Don't Do
✓ Take primary responsibility for meeting your own publication goals. ✓ Give byline credit to any attorney (associate, staff attorney, or summer intern) who makes a meaningful contribution to an article (e.g., >25 percent of its text).	✗ Rely upon another attorney to accomplish your article-writing goals. ✗ Coauthor short articles.

SECTION III

Additional Considerations

CHAPTER 13

Deviating from the Rules

What you must learn is that these rules are no different from
the rules of a computer system. Some of them can be bent,
others can be broken.

—The Matrix

I started this book by explaining that the rules discussed in Section II are distillations of lessons that I have learned from trial and error over the years as I developed my own techniques for expertise-driven marketing and article writing. While they have served me well, and I believe that they can be used by many attorneys to improve the effectiveness of their articles, they are not the Ten Commandments and shouldn't be treated as such. In other words, there is no sin in breaking them. Indeed, I often find myself engaged in an article-writing topic that I know violates one or more of the rules. The important thing in terms of my own development as an author is that I *know* that I am violating a rule as I draft such an article; in other words, I am aware of what generally works, but I sometimes make conscious decisions to deviate from the tried-and-true rules.

There are many reasons to deviate from the rules. Here are just a few:

- *Evolution.* At the end of the day, most learning still happens through trial and error. If you don't break a rule once in a while, you can't tell if the rule still works and/ or if there is another, better rule out there.
- *Other purposes.* I find myself breaking rules most often when I have a purpose for writing that is not strictly for business development. For example, recently one of my former associates asked me to coauthor an article in

a magazine. As someone who follows the rules in this book near-religiously, I had an initial Pavlovian aversion, as the publication that he envisioned violated multiple rules—it was not efficiently structured (Rule 1: Efficient Writing), it was not short (Rule 2: Short), it had little ability to be repurposed (Rule 5: Recycling and the Rule of Threes), and it involved coordinated drafting (Rule 8: Do It Yourself). After thinking about it and using my conscious mind to push down my reflexive views on article writing, I said yes. Supporting a former colleague who shows initiative to write on a topic and wants to collaborate is, without a doubt, the right thing to do, regardless of whether the project is the most efficient use of time.

- *Interest.* Sometimes we write on a topic simply because we have an interest in the topic. That interest may drive us to do things that we might not otherwise do, such as write a long article (Rule 2: Short) or write on a topic that might be academically or personally interesting but have little obvious business-practical impact (Rule 3: Business Practical).

- *Rule inconsistency.* Not every topic, writing style, or publication is "built" to satisfy all the rules. I run into this often when I am reviewing the articles of other people. Often an article is simply not drafted in a way that could satisfy all the rules. If I were starting from scratch, I might approach the article differently, but when an article already exists, the perfect can become the enemy of the good. In other words, often articles can be improved by applying a couple of the rules without necessarily having to follow all of the rules.

CHAPTER 14

Goal Setting

Setting goals is the first step in turning the invisible into the visible.

—*Tony Robbins*

In the discussion of Rule 7 (Repetition and Stockpiling), I talked about how to increase the quantity of articles written by focusing on reachable goals (e.g., publishing one article a month) and then increasing the cadence of article writing in the short term (e.g., in January moving to a biweekly or weekly publication cycle) and then stockpiling articles to naturally increase the overall frequency with which you publish. While the technique of repetition and stockpiling is a tactic for increasing the frequency with which you publish, it does not answer the question that many people ask, which is "How many articles should I strive to publish in a year?"

I suppose if you were looking for a simple answer, it would be "Publish as many as you want to." That, of course, does not get to the heart of what most people are really asking, which is "How many articles should I strive to publish in a year in order to achieve my goal?"

To answer that question, it's important to first understand your goal and then decide on a strategy and a tactic that you think will help you accomplish your goal.

When it comes to discussing goals, strategies, and tactics, it's important to note that different people use those terms in different ways and that a common lexicon can be helpful.

When I use the term "goal," I am referring to what you want the outcome to be. So, for example, a goal might be to be recognized as having expertise in your field, to increase the size of your practice, or to generate new clients. It describes the end state that you aspire to but have not yet achieved.

When I use the term "strategy," I am referring to your hypothesis as to what tangible action or achievement might accomplish your goal. For example, if your goal is to be recognized as having expertise in your field, your strategy might be to become one of the top ten published authors in that field. It is a relatively tangible accomplishment (i.e., you can test whether you have become one of the top ten published authors) and has a reasonable relationship to achieving the motivating goal of being recognized for expertise.

While having a strategy is important because it gives you something tangible to work toward, it does not suggest what you need to do in order to get there. That is where a tactic comes in. A tactic describes the specific tangible steps that will accomplish your strategy. Going back to the example in the previous paragraph, if your goal is to be recognized as having expertise in your field, and your strategy is to become one of the top ten published authors, you might research who the current frequently published or cited authors are in your field and get a sense of what has pushed them to their level of recognition. For example, if two or three attorneys are ranked in your field as the greatest "thought leaders" or the most read authors (see Rule 6: Metrics) or are simply cited by numerous sources and publications, look up how many articles they published in the past year and what types of topics they wrote about. If you find out that the author who is currently cited as the top thought leader in your area published 30 times last year, your tactic might be to publish 30 times in the coming year on topics that you believe are just as interesting (or, hopefully, even more interesting).

- Your **goal** would be to become recognized on your expertise in your field.
- Your **strategy** would be to gain the recognition by becoming one of the top ten published authors.
- Your **tactic** would be to publish 30 efficient (Rule 1), short (Rule 2), business-practical (Rule 3), and shelf-stable (Rule 4) articles in a year.

In comparison, if your goal is to develop new business from existing clients, you might find yourself coming to a different conclusion. Your strategy in that case might be to periodically and methodically reach out to your existing clients on a topical issue to stay top of mind. Your tactic might be to send all of your clients a publication at least once a month to gently remind them of your expertise in the area that you wish to market. In other words:

- Your **goal** would be to develop additional work from your existing clients.
- Your **strategy** would be to remind them on a consistent basis of your expertise.
- Your **tactic** would be to stockpile 12 articles (Rule 7) and e-mail them on the first Monday of every month so that your clients never go more than four weeks without seeing your name and being reminded of your expertise and availability to help.

CHAPTER 15

Developing Expertise

Nothing leads so straight to futility as literary ambitions without systematic knowledge.

—H.G. Wells

A central assumption throughout this book is that the reader has expertise in a field and that their goal is to market their expertise by communicating implicitly to clients and future clients that they are the "best" in their field. Many attorneys are not, however, experts in their field; or, if they are experts in their field, they may not have reached the level in their practice where they themselves believe that they are the best. So too, for those who have gained the confidence that they are practicing at the top of their craft, that confidence is often limited to specific areas of practice. Put differently, even the "best" recognize that they are not the "best" at all things and continually practice to deepen and broaden their knowledge base.

While expertise-driven marketing is often focused on the goal of building a practice and obtaining new and interesting work, it can have a secondary purpose of fitting into the broader picture of helping to develop your overall expertise as part of your practice development.

When it comes to the practice development of an attorney who is expertise-oriented, I strive for what I refer to as BIC POV—the *Best in Class Point of View*. What does that mean? It is a point of view about an issue, project, matter, policy, procedure, or problem that you believe is better than the points of view expressed by the average attorney in your field and rivals the points of view that might be shared by those attorneys whom you consider to be among the elites.

How do you get there? Sometimes BIC POVs grow organically. You find yourself addressing the same issue repeatedly throughout your career, and, at some point, you sit back and introspectively realize that you have developed a point of view that may be unique or, at a minimum, may be more informed by experience and knowledge than the points of view that might be held by other attorneys who come to the issue fresh (or at least less frequently). Growing a BIC POV organically, however, is like growing flowers on your front lawn. You don't necessarily intend to have them, you kind of are surprised when they bloom, you don't complain or mow them down, but nor do you have any idea how they got there or how to make more.

If you want to develop BIC POVs, I would suggest not just waiting for them to appear. At the risk of overdoing the previous metaphor—if you want flowers, start a garden; don't just wait for blooms in your lawn.

Developing a BIC POV is a lot like developing a product or a service in other industries. You can intentionally, systematically, and purposefully create one. When you look at how businesses and other industries create products, you find numerous methodologies that are designed to expedite and replicate the creation process. Specific methodologies are selected in other industries to account for a variety of factors. These include the type of product envisioned, the complexity of the development process, the size of the team attempting the development, and the speed at which development must occur.

Take, for example, software engineering. There are several software development life cycles that have been developed over the years. One of the most well-known is the waterfall technique.

The waterfall technique refers to a process in which the development of software happens in sequential phases that flow from one to the other—i.e., flow down like a waterfall. For example, in phase 1, specifications might be drafted that address the requirements of a particular piece of software. In phase 2, the software is designed. In phase 3, the software is implemented, in phase 4 it is tested, and in phase 5 it is deployed. The waterfall system relies upon faith that each step in the process was completed well. That faith means that developers are discouraged from revising or revisiting prior phases. Once one phase is complete (e.g., requirements), the results of that phase are locked in stone so that all attention can shift to the next phase. The waterfall technique could be applied, by analogy, when developing a BIC POV in your practice. Consider the following phases:

1. *Phase 1 BIC POV memorialization*: A partner/counsel puts together a checklist that identifies the issues that they believe comprise a best-in-class point of view with regard to a particular policy. The checklist serves three purposes: (1) it forms a discussion draft for socializing the BIC POV around the team, (2) it forms an internal checklist that can be used to issue-spot against a client's practice or policy and provide to the client an explanation of any gaps and your BIC POV, and (3) once perfected, it allows the BIC POV to be executed by others on the team (i.e., associates can use the validation checklist as guidance).

2. *Phase 2 BIC POV consensus*: The partner/counsel circulates the validation checklist to two to three other subject-matter experts for feedback and additional issue-spotting (i.e., what is missing from the checklist?).

3. *Phase 3 BIC template*: The partner/counsel drafts a policy or procedure (or adapts a current policy or procedure) that comports with the validation checklist. Put differently, you create a document template from the validation checklist and/or self-validate an existing template against your checklist.

4. *Phase 4 BIC template consensus*: The template is circulated to two to three internal subject-matter experts for feedback and adaptation.

5. *Phase 5 BIC product finalization*: The validation checklist and template are circulated to a larger team for execution by other attorneys and associates.

6. *Phase 6 BIC POV soft marketing*: A series of short (300-word) articles are spun off of the validation checklist, either as self-published FAQs or "top five consideration" pieces. Those articles might be designed to be serialized (e.g., bound as a "Top Ten FAQs," etc.) to explain the BIC POV.

7. *Phase 7 BIC direct marketing*: Direct marketing collateral is drafted that describes and defines the approach and assigns pricing for execution to the extent feasible.

CHAPTER 16

Choosing Your Area of Expertise

The successful warrior is the average man, with laser-like focus.

—*Bruce Lee*

Many attorneys who read this book already have practices that focus on a particular legal area or a particular industry (e.g., labor and employment, antitrust, government contracts, etc.). Some readers, however, may have a practice that focuses on a very broad area of law to which expertise marketing may not be conducive (e.g., corporate law or commercial litigation). If you are in the latter camp but are interested in building a practice through expertise-driven marketing, you may be asking yourself the very existential question "What expertise should I choose?" While attorneys of any age may find themselves facing that question, for younger readers (e.g., one to four years out of law school), the "what expertise should I choose" question is often real, imminent, and reoccurring.

It is well beyond the scope of this book to guide you through all of the variables and considerations that attorneys take into account when they decide which area of law to focus on. That said, many attorneys do (and all attorneys arguably should) take into consideration whether a particular area of expertise that they are considering is conducive to expertise-driven marketing.

There is no single "right way" for that consideration to factor into the greater career soul-searching process. To put it differently, it's not as simple as saying that when you are a third-year associate, you need to ask yourself, "Does my area of intended expertise allow for expertise-driven marketing?" The reason is simple—all attorneys take different paths toward developing expertise. Take for example the following descriptions of three expertise-driven attorneys and their career development.

First, I'll describe my own journey toward expertise-driven marketing.

Like most attorneys, I did not come out of law school knowing that I wanted to focus on a particular area of law—let alone that I wanted my practice to be entirely focused on data privacy and data security. Even if I had an inkling that I wanted to focus my practice (and I did not at that stage), the fields of data privacy and data security did not exist when I went to law school. Instead, I joined an Am Law 100 law firm as a commercial litigation associate. I thought, at the time, that I might like litigating cases and that I would enjoy learning the broad skill set that litigators use as part of their craft.

Well, I did enjoy the broad skill sets that I was exposed to, but I also found that I did not enjoy that with every new case and every new project, I felt like I was starting over by having to research an area of law from ground zero as if I was a brand-new attorney. What I was beginning to realize is that I enjoyed concentrating my practice in a single area so that I had a body of legal knowledge that I could tap into when a client called. In other words, I realized that I wanted to focus my practice on one area and develop expertise.

Realizing the benefits of developing expertise, of course, is one part of the equation. It does not, however, provide any indication as to what area of law to develop. At that time, I had handled antitrust cases, personal injury cases, commercial disputes, human resources disputes, and consumer protection cases. Any one of those could be an area of focus. I chose antitrust because I found it the most intellectually stimulating, and, for the next three years, I became an antitrust litigation associate. While I enjoyed the practice and the intellectual stimulation, I found business development to be extremely difficult. Specifically, the field of antitrust attorneys was huge (i.e., antitrust has been around for a hundred years and some of its practitioners are nearly that old!). It was difficult, if not impossible, as a young attorney to position myself as the "best" antitrust attorney, or even the "best" in the subclass of antitrust litigation. I was simply one of many. From an article-writing perspective, I also found myself drawn to articles and topics that were interesting to fellow antitrust attorneys but tended to be esoteric, academic, and non–business practical.

I made a conscious decision to shift my practice away from antitrust litigation toward advertising litigation. My motivation for doing so was fairly simple. There were fewer advertising litigation attorneys than antitrust attorneys (at least at that time), and I had a better sense of how I could distinguish myself in terms of offering business-practical advice to clients. While my career progressed, and flourished, with that greater degree of specialization, over time I realized two things. First, advertising law was functionally stagnant in terms of business growth. There was functionally the same number of cases filed year over year. The pie was not growing. Second, the advertising defense bar was developed and mature; i.e., it was still difficult to distinguish myself as the "best" in the field.

I made a conscious decision to narrow my focus to a particular area within advertising law. I was looking for a subspecialty that was in a growth phase in terms of demand (i.e., increasing pie) and for which either the legal bar was not well developed (i.e., short supply) or there was still room to become a "best in class" attorney. At the time, data privacy and data security were still not recognized as formal legal fields but rather as a small subset of the larger field of advertising law (from a regulatory standpoint, the focus of data privacy and data security law was advertising misrepresentations companies made about their privacy and security practices). Having handled many privacy and security matters, I decided to focus my practice, my article writing, and my business development into what, at the time, was perceived as a microniche. Over time, that microniche grew well beyond the confines of advertising law into its own field that itself has spun off dozens of microniches (e.g., health care privacy law, data breach response, European data privacy law, government contractor security and privacy obligations, etc.).

My experience differs from that of other expertise-driven attorneys. Take one of my colleagues with a highly successful community banking practice. In law school, he did a clerkship for the Department of Justice, which provided him enough exposure to litigation for him to decide that was not his cup of tea. At the time, his understanding was that if you were not going to litigate, you became a "corporate" lawyer doing business transactions.

When he applied to law firms for a second-year summer associate position, he was accepted at a prestigious regional firm that utilized a "rotation" system wherein summer associates were exposed to a number of different practice areas. By luck, one of his rotational areas was banking. He thought that the work was okay, but he really liked the attorneys in the practice and was excited when he got an offer to join as a full-time associate. While he stayed at the same firm, and in the same practice, for the entirety of his career, he realized that the term "banking attorney" meant a lot of different things to different people. Some banking attorneys specialized in dealing with bank regulators (e.g., the CFPB, the OCC, the Federal Reserve). Indeed, some banking attorneys focused on dealing with a single specific bank regulator (i.e., just the Federal Reserve). Other banking attorneys assisted in mergers and acquisitions, others in consumer litigation, and still others in the development of new banking products. In addition to legal areas of subspecialization, different sectors of the banking industry faced different concerns and issues. For example, a top-five bank might have a hundred in-house attorneys. A community bank, on the other hand, might have no in-house attorney. The legal needs of a big bank and a community bank are very different. Trying to be the "best" banking attorney—or to sell himself as the "best" banking attorney—felt like an impossible task.

He decided to focus his practice on one particular industry sector—community banks. He also decided to focus his article writing on the same sector. While he wrote on all manner of banking issues, and many of the articles that he wrote (and much of his expertise) might have equal applicability to a top-five bank, each of his articles was oriented toward the business-practical impact that a particular issue would have on a community bank. In other words, the "spin" of his article writing was always community bank focused. If he goes to a conference today with a thousand banking lawyers, while he might hesitate to say that he is the "best" banking lawyer in the room, he is unequivocally recognized as the best (or one of the best) *community* banking attorneys in the room.

As a third example, another colleague began his practice at a top silk-stocking law firm moving between practice groups. He realized that he wanted to focus on a particular legal area to gain expertise and decided that, in order to do so, he needed to switch law firms. He had some exposure to environmental law and enjoyed the practice so decided to accept a position at another law firm in their environmental law group. At the time, he considered environmental law a good area of focus because it touched upon a variety of different industry groups and would allow him to meet partners from across the firm as he helped with their clients' various environmental matters. For the first part of his career, he did not focus much on expertise-driven marketing and, instead, relied on the fact that environmental law was in a rapid demand growth phase—i.e., the pie was growing quickly as dozens of new environmental laws and regulations came online. During the second phase of his career, however, the demand for environmental law stabilized as fewer new laws were enacted and the pool of attorneys with deep environmental experience grew. Although he already had a successful environmental law practice, he decided to pivot his business development efforts toward expertise-driven marketing and article writing.

As he began that pivot, he realized how difficult it was to stand out in the field of environmental lawyers. Specifically, environmental law had grown to a size and complexity such that not only were there thousands of environmental lawyers across the country, but subspecialties had also developed around particular issues such as clean water, clean air, recyclables, land pollution, etc. It simply was not possible or realistic to be identified as the "best" environmental lawyer. The field was too broad. Instead, he realized that if he was going to be identified as the best, or one of the best, practitioners, he needed to focus his efforts on a particular area of law. In other words, while it might be impossible for any one person to say that they are the best environmental lawyer, a person could be the best nanotechnology lawyer or the best bio-based plastics lawyer. His article-writing efforts started to evolve from general environmental topics toward specific industries and specific environmental issues.

These three vignettes show some areas of divergence and some areas of commonality. In terms of areas of divergence, each attorney began focusing on a particular area of law for a different reason. Some because they found an area of law academically interesting, others because they received a job offer to join a practice in that area or because they saw the business rationale for specialization.

In terms of similarities, at some point in each attorney's career development, they began to think about their area of expertise through the lens of business development and specifically business development through article writing. When that happened, it fundamentally shaped their career progression. In my case, it led me to switch my area of focus completely from antitrust to advertising and consumer protection. In other cases, it caused a less dramatic decision to stay within the same area of law but begin to focus on a particular industry segment. For example, to go from being a banking attorney to a *community* banking attorney. It also led to an explicit or implicit recognition that the "goal" when choosing an area to focus upon was to find an area in which the attorney could work toward being and ultimately be perceived as the "best" in the field. In all three examples, that meant progressively finding a narrower and narrower focus until a niche was identified that could be legitimately mastered.

It's important to note that for each of the attorneys above, they started general (e.g., corporate lawyer or litigator) and slowly worked their way into progressively narrower areas of focus (e.g., banking attorney and then community banking attorney, or consumer protection attorney and then data privacy attorney). The process of going from the broad to the narrow takes time, and sometimes it can't be short-circuited.

I often see attorneys decide that they want to focus on a particular area of expertise and inadvertently choose a microniche that may be too small to be relevant or too small to support a practice. For example, if a corporate attorney decided one day that they wanted to focus on an area and rebrand themselves as a drone-delivery attorney, that might be a microniche comprised of only one or two potential clients. Instead, the journey of progressively narrowing a practice is sometimes needed in order to find the right balance of expertise versus microniche. In the example above, it might be more realistic to begin to focus on transportation and logistics legal issues and to get a sense of whether articles will, over time, position them as the go-to person for the logistics industry. If the answer is that the industry is not well defined or is inundated with practitioners and different subsegments, then explore whether automated logistics might be a better level of specialization.

To summarize, if you are in the process of thinking about choosing an area of law or industry to focus upon, the following factors are worth considering:

- Is the demand for an area of practice in a growth phase (i.e., is the pie growing)?
- Is the supply of legal practitioners in the area of practice mature, developed, and stable (i.e., stagnant)?
- Is there a realistic possibility that you can become one of the best practitioners in the area and through expertise-driven marketing be perceived as one of the best practitioners in the area?
- If not, is there a narrower niche in which you might become one of the best practitioners in the niche and through expertise-driven marketing be perceived as one of the best practitioners in the niche?
- Is the niche that you are considering a microniche such that there may not be a sufficient number of potential clients to support a practice?

CHAPTER 17

Campaigns

There are a few moments in every game when I will have to sprint and use my explosiveness to win.

—Ali Krieger

Rule 7 (Repetition and Stockpiling) discusses the concept of stockpiling articles in order to spread publications out throughout the year. If you follow Rule 7, you will ensure that you are continually publishing and that clients, and potential clients, continually see your name associated with your area of expertise.

While I follow Rule 7 with regard to the vast majority of my articles, sometimes there is a reason to deviate from the rule. In other words, instead of filtering articles out over time from my stockpile, I may decide to draft a series of articles and then to strategically release them all at once (or release them sequentially in a series day after day).

When does it make sense to intentionally flood the market with content around an issue as a sort of issue-centered campaign? Campaigns are most effective if there is a new law or regulation that you believe will have a long-term impact in your area of practice. When that occurs, there is a narrow window in which you have a unique opportunity to establish your expertise before other attorneys can establish theirs.

Typically, when a new law is passed, nobody has written substantively about the new issue. Indeed, most other attorneys are focused on newscasting, which serves only to inform clients and potential clients of the *existence* of the new law; they are not focused on writing shelf-stable content (Rule 4) that goes beyond explaining the existence of the law and addresses actionable, realistic, and beneficial takeaways from the law (Rule 3). In those circumstances, if you can produce a large quantity of high-quality, short (Rule 2), business-practical (Rule 3), and shelf-stable (Rule 4) articles, there may be a strategic reason to do so, as you can quickly establish yourself as one of the only attorneys (if not the only attorney) with the type of expertise that businesses are searching for and that other attorneys lack. I call those situations in which you effectively try to flood the market with content a "campaign." Campaigns often go beyond publications and may combine publications with speaking, webinars, and other forms of expertise-driven marketing, all focused on establishing you as an expert in the area in a fast, effective, and long-lasting manner.

CHAPTER 18

Identifying Good Publication Sources

If it's not immediately apparent why your story belongs in the publication to which you're pitching, clarify that now.

—*Haidn Ellis Foster (freelance writer)*

Thanks in large part to the Internet, most legal publishing has shifted from writing for established journals, magazines, and newsletters to self-publishing, either on a law firm website or through social media channels. From my perspective, that trend is a net positive. It allows outside counsel to publish more content, with fewer intermediaries, and it ensures that in-house counsel have access to exponentially more content than was available 20 years ago, when all articles had to go through editorial boards and committees.

While the vast majority of articles today are self-published, that does not necessarily mean that you should never publish with third parties. Well-respected publications can, if done correctly, add a level of trust and prestige to not only your article but also your name. In some respects, they function like "trust brands"—they convey to the reader that an outside board of experts has already considered your article and your ideas and found them to be worthy of general consumption.

Picking the right publications to work with, however, is essential. As discussed in Rule 2 (Short), there is a real cost to choosing the wrong publication, as it can lead you to expend substantially more time publishing a single article when the opportunity cost of doing so may be dozens of smaller articles that are more likely to reach their intended audience.

When deciding whether a publication is the right outlet for your content, consider applying the first six rules to the publication—not just to the article that you are considering writing. The following provides a checklist of things to think about by rule:

Rule 1: Efficient Writing. Many publications have editorial requirements that may cause you to deviate from the efficient structure that you created under Rule 1. For example, a journal or a newsletter may ask that you provide a general overview of the law, that you include a certain number of footnotes, or that you change your tone and style to something that you are not familiar with and, hence, will cause you additional time to adapt your writing. In general, try to identify publications that already match your efficient writing style to minimize the need to make modifications that may cost time and energy.

Rule 2: Short. The hallmark of Rule 2 is to keep your articles short and to the point. If one of the editorial requirements for a particular journal, newsletter, or media outlet is a large word count, before agreeing to publish, ask yourself how many short articles you could self-publish as an alternative.

Rule 3: Business Practical. The most prestigious publications are often *not* those that focus on business-practical articles. As a result, the type of people who may read the prestigious publication may not be the type of practical in-house counsel whom you are trying to reach. Remember that you are no longer in law school; if your goal is to develop business, you are not trying to publish a note in the law review—you are trying to be read by in-house counsel. If you are uncertain about whether a particular publication is read by in-house counsel, simply ask. Call up one of your colleagues or friends who is in-house and ask them if they read the publication that you are considering and, if so, how often.

Rule 4: Shelf Stable. In the context of publications, shelf stable does not refer to whether or not the content of articles will be relevant but whether a potential reader will be able to easily find the publication weeks or months after your article comes out. For example, if a publication is a print-only magazine that is not electronically indexed, any article that is written for the publication has a short shelf life (i.e., the time between when the magazine is received and when it finds itself in the recycle bin). Conversely, if a publication is archived and housed online, then it would be considered shelf stable, as potential readers should be able to find your article long after it is released.

Rule 5: Recycling and the Rule of Threes. In the context of evaluating a publication, recycling and the rule of threes translates into whether you are permitted to reuse and republish your article. If the publication will own the copyright to your article, or if you are granting the publication an exclusive and irrevocable license, then you will not have an opportunity to reuse and recycle your article in the future. Conversely, if you will retain the copyright to your article and you grant the publication only a nonexclusive license, then you may be free to repurpose, republish, and reuse your content. In terms of Rule 5, be very wary of legal publications that post your article only once, behind a paywall (i.e., subscribers only), and prevent you from reusing and republicizing your own material.

Rule 6: Metrics. Finally, while it is not typically a deal breaker if they cannot, some publications are able to provide you with metrics concerning not only their average readership but also the specific readership of your article. Choosing a publication that is able to provide you with quantitative feedback concerning the effectiveness and penetration of your article is always a plus.

In addition to applying the preceding six rules, also consider the following two factors. First, steer toward publications that have low "friction" in terms of going from draft manuscript to final product. Publications that require multiple submissions, tendering of primary materials used in an article, or working with editorial boards can consume an inordinate amount of time. Second, steer toward publications that have fast turnaround times. If you have followed Rule 4 (Shelf Stable), it's not essential that your article come out a week or two after you submit it to the publication. That said, nobody wants to wait six months or a year to see their article in print. Even the best and most shelf-stable articles may find themselves stale if a year goes by.

CHAPTER 19

Social Media

Social media replaces nothing, but complements everything.

—Neal Schaffer (social media consultant)

Social media can be a tool for developing business in its own right. As this book is focused on traditional article writing, it does not endeavor to talk about the art of conducting expertise-driven marketing through social media posts, developing followers, contributing to topical news groups, and writing articles in 140 characters or less. Expertise-driven marketing through social media is probably a topic worthy of a book unto itself. That said, and without focusing on the art of utilizing social media as its own method of promoting expertise, social media can be a tool for distributing and publicizing your articles.

To understand how social media can interact with your article writing, think of business development as a marketing funnel. At the top of the funnel, your goal is to make a pool of potential clients aware of your existence. After a large pool of potential clients have awareness of who you are (i.e., recognize your name), the goal is to get some subset of that population to consider whether you might be a good resource for them. Among that smaller group, some percentage of them will become clients, and then the business development effort pivots toward maintaining them as a client, exposing them to more of what you have to offer, and (hopefully) growing the type of projects that they ask you to work on.

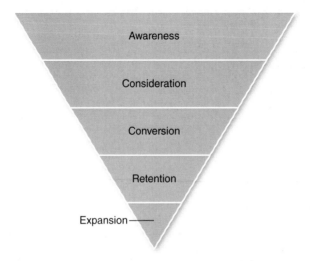

I would argue that article writing supports almost every aspect of the marketing funnel. Your articles build brand awareness and name recognition, they are designed to make potential clients consider you as a potential resource, they hopefully support and lead to new clients, and they help retain and expand existing clients by continually reminding them of your area of expertise and exposing them to new ways in which you can support them. Social media can support this process by helping to bring awareness to your articles (and through your articles to you). In that respect, social media can be a tool to publicize and distribute your articles, even if it is not a strategy unto itself for getting a potential client to consider you, retain you, or continue to use you.

How best can social media be leveraged to act as a tool for bringing awareness to you and to your articles? I would consider the following four suggestions.

First, don't rely upon a social media platform as your medium for article writing. In other words, your article should have a home that is not on the social media platform. The social media post should link to your article but not *be* your article. The reason is simple. Social media posts tend not to be indexed by major search engines and tend, over time, to be lost as most social media platforms focus on displaying the most recent posts. You want to ensure that your article is not lost in a timeline or news feed buried by years of articles, current events, and cat videos.

Second, most social media platforms function by sharing your content with other individuals who have opted in to see your news feed or to follow you. How your content is shared, however, differs by platform. It may be mixed in with hundreds of posts that came out at around the same time, or it may be highlighted via the social media platform's algorithms as being particularly relevant to a subset of your followers. In either case, whether someone actually sees your article depends upon whether they are using the social media platform at a time that you publish and at a place in which they are capable of (and interested in) reading your article. The percentage of your own contacts who fit those criteria may be relatively small (e.g., 10 percent). To go beyond that universe, you need them to share your article with others.

Whether a contact shares an article depends in part upon whether they like your article. It also depends on whether they are thinking about sharing it at the time they read it. Don't be afraid to make them think about it by asking them to share it or post it. If you publish a large volume of articles, you can't, of course, get in the habit of asking your contacts every day to share your articles, but if you have a particular article that you think demonstrates your expertise, simply ask in a post if they will share it with their contacts. In that regard, don't be afraid to be blunt. For example, you could privately message particular contacts and explain that you are trying to get publicity around a certain topic: "Hi John! Hope all is going well. I wrote an article about X and was trying to get the word out that this is an area of law I know a lot about. Could I ask you to share the article with your connections?" You could also ask all of your contacts to share the article: "Just published on a fascinating and not well understood topic that impacts businesses. Would appreciate it if you would 'share' it to help get the word out."

Third, people tend to have the lowest attention spans when navigating social media platforms. That is due in part to the fact that social media is predominantly accessed via smartphones on small screens; it's also due to the fact that people often check social media when they have small breaks and are not fully engaged in work-related issues (e.g., standing in line, waiting for the doctor, riding a bus or subway). Reduced attention span means it's even more important than normal to quickly grab their attention and convey to them that your article is business practical (Rule 3). There are many ways to do this. For example, make sure that your article is visually appealing. If a social media platform allows you to post a picture, do so and make sure that the picture is not a stock photo of your logo or your headshot. Try to find something eye catching and engaging. Also make sure that your title is short and to the point and conveys the topic to which the article relates.

Fourth, many social media platforms give preference when displaying posts to those that have garnered significant interactions from other users. Interaction in this context could be "likes" or "thumbs up," but it could also be comments. Encourage readers to comment on your article by introducing a question into the article that asks readers to give their reaction. Be careful not to ask too much of readers. Per the previous paragraph, remember that most readers of social media have low attention spans, so it is not the time to ask a reader to write a well-drafted essay responding to your thesis. Instead, ask them to do something small, easy, and quick. For example, you could ask readers to post comments about their experience with a topic, or you could ask them to comment about whether there are any other issues they think are relevant to the topic. You could do something even simpler and ask them to "thumbs up" the article if they have run into the issue before or if they have had someone ask them a similar question. The focus of social media is, after all, to be *social*. Readers tend to like to engage with content on social media if a relatively easy ask is made of them.

APPENDIX A

Practice Identifying Popular Article Titles

PRACTICE SHEET 1

Test your ability to identify what titles would appeal to readers. Next to each article title below, write whether you think that the article would get high, low, or average readership. Once you are done, compare your answers to the actual readership on page 197:

Title	Readership
A €150k warning to employers - don't ask your employees to consent to your privacy policy!	
An Additional Step towards the Modernization of Control of Mergers in France	
Arbitration, Mediation, and the Singapore Convention on Mediation	
Babies, Bodies and Borders: The Risks and Rise of Surrogacy	
Biting off more than you can chew: no oral modification and entire agreement clauses	
Brexit: a change of direction on protection of UK worker rights?	
California Consumer Privacy Act (CCPA) - Answers to the Most Frequently Asked Questions Concerning Cookies and AdTech	
California Employers Have Less Than Six Months To Complete Sexual Harassment and Abusive Conduct Training	
CCPA Privacy FAQs: Can a company decide whether to deidentify information or delete information if it receives a 'right to be forgotten' request?	
CCPA Privacy FAQs: Does the CCPA apply to personal data about non-Californians (e.g., Europeans)?	
CCPA Privacy FAQs: How far can a company go to validate the identity of an individual making a data subject access request?	

continued

continued

Title	Readership
Client alert: the French Supreme Court validates the "Macron Grid" which caps damages awarded to employees in cases of unfair dismissal	
CMA Publishes Digital Markets Strategy	
EU Commission Hits Qualcomm with Fine of EUR 242 million for Predatory Pricing	
Family Asset Protection - LGBT* clients and alternative families	
French Gender Equality Index	
New CNIL Guidelines on Cookies and Tracking Devices	
New Regulations for Charitable Contributions in Exchange for State or Local Tax Credits	
Off-Payroll Working Rules	
Prudential's £12bn transfer of annuity policies to Rothesay blocked by the High Court	
Quantum meruit - how much is too much?	
SEC Proposes Amendments to Financial Information Reporting Requirements for Acquired and Disposed Business	
Sixth Circuit Holds Nonmember of Credit Union Lacks Standing to Bring ADA Claim Based on Allegedly Inaccessible Website	
Technology v the law: The future of E-signatures in Real Estate	
Trump Administration Targets Government of Venezuela in Expanded Sanctions	
U.S. Supreme Court Limits Judicial Deference To Administrative Agency Interpretation of Their Own Ambiguous Rules	
What Do Employers Need to Do to Accommodate Nursing Mothers?	
What Employers Need to Know about New York State's New Discrimination and Harassment Laws: Part 2	
Would you make contact with a hacker with a view to making payment?	

Actual readership

Title	Readership	Comparison to Average*
A €150k warning to employers - don't ask your employees to consent to your privacy policy!	High	392.77%
An Additional Step towards the Modernization of Control of Mergers in France	Low	21.69%
Arbitration, Mediation, and the Singapore Convention on Mediation	Average	130.12%
Babies, Bodies and Borders: The Risks and Rise of Surrogacy	Average	107.23%
Biting off more than you can chew: no oral modification and entire agreement clauses	High	569.28%
Brexit: a change of direction on protection of UK worker rights?	Average	113.25%
California Consumer Privacy Act (CCPA) - Answers to the Most Frequently Asked Questions Concerning Cookies and AdTech	High	347.59%
California Employers Have Less Than Six Months To Complete Sexual Harassment and Abusive Conduct Training	High	322.29%
CCPA Privacy FAQs: Can a company decide whether to deidentify information or delete information if it receives a 'right to be forgotten' request?	High	450.00%
CCPA Privacy FAQs: Does the CCPA apply to personal data about non-Californians (e.g., Europeans)?	High	359.04%
CCPA Privacy FAQs: How far can a company go to validate the identity of an individual making a data subject access request?	High	493.98%
Client alert: the French Supreme Court validates the "Macron Grid" which caps damages awarded to employees in cases of unfair dismissal	Low	24.70%
CMA Publishes Digital Markets Strategy	Low	40.36%
EU Commission Hits Qualcomm with Fine of EUR 242 million for Predatory Pricing	Low	61.45%
Family Asset Protection - LGBT* clients and alternative families	Low	43.98%
French Gender Equality Index	Low	43.98%

continued

continued

Title	Readership	Comparison to Average*
New CNIL Guidelines on Cookies and Tracking Devices	Average	106.63%
New Regulations for Charitable Contributions in Exchange for State or Local Tax Credits	Low	28.92%
Off-Payroll Working Rules	Average	104.82%
Prudential's £12bn transfer of annuity policies to Rothesay blocked by the High Court	Low	66.27%
Quantum meruit - how much is too much?	High	327.11%
SEC Proposes Amendments to Financial Information Reporting Requirements for Acquired and Disposed Business	Low	35.54%
Sixth Circuit Holds Nonmember of Credit Union Lacks Standing to Bring ADA Claim Based on Allegedly Inaccessible Website	Low	46.99%
Technology v the law: The future of E-signatures in Real Estate	High	281.93%
Trump Administration Targets Government of Venezuela in Expanded Sanctions	Average	90.96%
U.S. Supreme Court Limits Judicial Deference To Administrative Agency Interpretation of Their Own Ambiguous Rules	Low	20.48%
What Do Employers Need to Do to Accommodate Nursing Mothers?	Average	121.08%
What Employers Need to Know about New York State's New Discrimination and Harassment Laws: Part 2	High	269.28%
Would you make contact with a hacker with a view to making payment?	High	301.20%

*Comparison is to the average readership of articles published by Am Law 100 firms in the third quarter of 2019 according to Lexology.

PRACTICE SHEET 2

Test your ability to identify what titles would appeal to readers. Next to each article title below, write whether you think that the article would get high, low, or average readership. Once you are done, compare your answers to the actual readership on page 201:

Title	Readership
2018 Bank M&A Statistics	
After Losing the Vote, Oil & Gas Opponents Try Litigation	
Avoiding Management Struggles When It Comes to Data Breaches: Part 5	
Brexit and Data Protection: "Deal or No Deal" Preparations	
Can a company be sued under the CCPA for using behavioral advertising?	
Do liquidated damages survive termination? (answer in no more than 1000 words)	
Does the "right to be forgotten" under the California Consumer Privacy Act require that companies delete the same type of information as the "right to be forgotten" under the GDPR?	
Effectiveness and efficiency of AIFMD under scrutiny	
Emerging Themes in Financial Regulation 2019—What do I need to know?	
EU & Competition Law Update—January 2019	
Georgia Senate Considers Expanding Scope of Eavesdropping Statute	
How Will a No-Deal Brexit Effect Merger Control	
HR Two Minute Monthly: discrimination; gender pay gap reporting; equal pay	
HR Two Minute Monthly: employment status; disability discrimination; collective redundancy	
IRS Releases March 2019 Interest Rates	
Land Value Capture in London: radicalism or another very British revolution?	
Mastercard Announces New Rules for Free Trials and Subscriptions (Effective April 2019)	

continued

continued

Title	Readership
Missouri Faces Challenge to Meat Labeling Law	
Myanmar Postcard—22 February 2019	
New IRS Addresses for Filing Estate and Gift Tax Returns	
Non Party PI Insurers Liable for Costs	
Public Forums Underway in California Consumer Privacy Act Rulemaking	
SMCR for FCA-solo regulated firms—how to survive implementation	
Statute of Limitations on Reverse Mortgages	
TE/GE Fiscal Year 2018 Accomplishments Letter	
The FCA has published Primary Market Bulletin No. 20	
The next Carillion? Do you have the right safeguards in your outsourcing contracts to protect your business?	
Trade Policy Tensions Emerge as U.S. Reimposes Sanctions against Iran (IRB No. 577)	
Vietnam Wind—A look ahead to 2019	
What Happens to My Digital Assets on Death or Incapacity?	

Actual readership

Title	Readership	Comparison to Average*
2018 Bank M&A Statistics	Low	21.08%
After Losing the Vote, Oil & Gas Opponents Try Litigation	Low	86.14%
Avoiding Management Struggles When It Comes to Data Breaches: Part 5	Average	116.27%
Brexit and Data Protection: "Deal or No Deal" Preparations	High	219.28%
Can a company be sued under the CCPA for using behavioral advertising?	High	416.87%
Do liquidated damages survive termination? (answer in no more than 1000 words)	High	572.89%
Does the "right to be forgotten" under the California Consumer Privacy Act require that companies delete the same type of information as the "right to be forgotten" under the GDPR?	High	303.61%
Effectiveness and efficiency of AIFMD under scrutiny	High	174.70%
Emerging Themes in Financial Regulation 2019—What do I need to know?	Average	149.40%
EU & Competition Law Update—January 2019	Average	136.75%
Georgia Senate Considers Expanding Scope of Eavesdropping Statute	Low	42.77%
How Will a No-Deal Brexit Effect Merger Control	Low	69.88%
HR Two Minute Monthly: discrimination; gender pay gap reporting; equal pay	Average	123.49%
HR Two Minute Monthly: employment status; disability discrimination; collective redundancy	High	284.94%
IRS Releases March 2019 Interest Rates	Low	17.47%
Land Value Capture in London: radicalism or another very British revolution?	High	286.14%
Mastercard Announces New Rules for Free Trials and Subscriptions (Effective April 2019)	High	274.70%
Missouri Faces Challenge to Meat Labeling Law	Low	33.13%
Myanmar Postcard—22 February 2019	Low	69.88%

continued

continued

Title	Readership	Comparison to Average*
New IRS Addresses for Filing Estate and Gift Tax Returns	High	159.64%
Non Party PI Insurers Liable for Costs	Average	100.00%
Public Forums Underway in California Consumer Privacy Act Rulemaking	Low	74.10%
SMCR for FCA-solo regulated firms—how to survive implementation	High	318.07%
Statute of Limitations on Reverse Mortgages	Average	140.96%
TE/GE Fiscal Year 2018 Accomplishments Letter	Low	13.86%
The FCA has published Primary Market Bulletin No. 20	Low	71.08%
The next Carillion? Do you have the right safeguards in your outsourcing contracts to protect your business?	Average	134.34%
Trade Policy Tensions Emerge as U.S. Reimposes Sanctions against Iran (IRB No. 577)	Low	86.14%
Vietnam Wind—A look ahead to 2019	Low	55.42%
What Happens to My Digital Assets on Death or Incapacity?	High	220.48%

*Comparison is to the average readership of articles published by Am Law 100 firms in the third quarter of 2019 according to Lexology.

APPENDIX B

Sample Article Structures

I. THE "OVERVIEW"

Template Structure

<table>
<tr><td colspan="3">Title: What In-House Counsel Need to Know about
<<INSERT TOPIC>>
<<INSERT PARAGRAPH DESCRIBING ISSUE>></td></tr>
<tr><td><<INSERT INTERESTING STATISTIC>></td><td><<INSERT INTERESTING STATISTIC>></td><td><<INSERT INTERESTING STATISTIC>></td></tr>
<tr><td><<INSERT INTERESTING STATISTIC>></td><td><<INSERT INTERESTING STATISTIC>></td><td><<INSERT INTERESTING STATISTIC>></td></tr>
<tr><td colspan="3">In-house counsel should consider the following when deciding upon a <<INSERT TOPIC>>
   <<INSERT CONSIDERATION 1>>
   <<INSERT CONSIDERATION 2>>
   <<INSERT CONSIDERATION 3>>
   <<INSERT CONSIDERATION 4>>
   <<INSERT CONSIDERATION 5>>
   . . .</td></tr>
</table>

Example of Its Application

What In-House Counsel Need to Know about Email Marketing

Email is ubiquitous in modern life with billions of emails—wanted and unwanted—sent each day. Since its enactment in 2003, the Controlling the Assault of Non-Solicited Pornography and Marketing ("CAN-SPAM") Act has attempted to curb the number of unwanted emails and impose some rules on a largely unregulated frontier. When followed, the CAN-SPAM Act's restrictions give email recipients some control over their inboxes and also maintain fairness in how emails present themselves. Failure to follow the CAN-SPAM Act can lead to penalties of up to $16,000 per violation.

As a practical matter, many organizations use vendors for their email marketing and other email services, and those vendors often assist the organizations in complying with the requirements of the CAN-SPAM Act. Nonetheless, the party whose content is promoted via email must supervise the conduct of its vendors and employees in abiding by CAN-SPAM, or else risk possible sanctions.

$44.00 Average return on each dollar of email marketing investment.[1]	246 Billion Projected number of daily business emails in 2020.[2]	244.5 Million Estimated number of email users in the US at the end of 2017.[3]	40% The percent of companies that offer BYOD to all employees.[4]

1. Allen Finn, *35 Face-Melting Email Marketing Stats for 2017*, WORDSTREAM BLOG (Dec. 21, 2017), https://www.wordstream.com/blog/ws/2017/06/29/email-marketing-statistics.
2. *Id.*
3. *Id.*
4. *Consumer Sentinel Network Data Book for January–December 2016*, FTC (Mar. 2017), https://www.ftc.gov/system/files/documents/reports/consumer-sentinel-network-data-book-january-december-2016/csn_cy-2016_data_book.pdf.

The basic questions to ask regarding CAN-SPAM compliance are:

1. Does your email message include: (a) complete and accurate transmission and header information; (b) a "From" line that identifies your business as the sender; (c) a "Subject" line that accurately describes your message; and (d) an effective "opt-out" mechanism?
2. Does your email either contain an email address, physical address, or other mechanism that the recipient may use for opting-out of future marketing emails?
3. Is your opt-out mechanism effective for at least 30 days after your email is sent?
4. Do you honor all requests to opt-out within 10 days?
5. Does your mailing list include any recipient that has asked not to receive email from your business (opted-out)?
6. Have you tested the effectiveness of your opt-out mechanism?
7. Have you reviewed your vendor contracts to determine each party's responsibilities with regard to CAN-SPAM compliance?
8. Are addresses of people that have opted-out transferred outside of your organization?
9. Does your organization use open relays or open proxies to send marketing email?
10. Have you validated your CAN-SPAM compliance program annually?

2. THE "FREQUENTLY ASKED QUESTION"
Template Structure

Title: <<INSERT>> *FAQ:* **<<INSERT QUESTION>>**

Answer:

<<INSERT SHORT ANSWER>>

<<INSERT EXPLANATION>>

<<COMMON SERIES SUMMARY>>

Example of Its Application

Privacy FAQ: Is a business required to implement a data breach Incident Response Plan ("IRP") under the California Consumer Privacy Act?

No.

    While the CCPA provides for statutory damages to California residents whose sensitive information is exposed in a data security breach, it does not expressly require a company to have a Data Breach Incident Response Plan ("IRP"). An IRP explains how an organization handles security incidents. Among other things, the plan helps employees from different departments understand the role that they are expected to play when investigating a security incident and identifies other people within the organization with whom they should be coordinating. The plan also can help educate employees concerning what they should and should not do when faced with a security incident and can provide them with a reference guide for resources that may help them effectively respond to an incident or breach.

    Although an organization is not required to have an IRP in place, a plaintiff pursuing statutory damages under the CCPA will need to prove that a company failed to implement and maintain reasonable and appropriate data security procedures and practices. In defending such a claim, it will be essential for a company to be able to identify such measures. An IRP will be helpful in establishing that the company took data security seriously and created a plan to quickly respond to a breach.

    In February 2016, California published the California Data Breach Report, in which it specifically identified the 20 controls set forth in the Center for Internet Security's Critical Security Controls ("CIS") as the "minimum level of security" an organization should meet.[1] Indeed, the report states that the "failure to implement all of the Controls that apply to an organization's environment constitutes a lack of reasonable security." Number 19 on the CIS Critical Security Controls is "Incident Response and Management." Thus, having an IRP will provide useful evidence to establish the company complied with CIS.

* * *

    This article is part of a multi-part series published by BCLP to help companies understand and implement the General Data Protection Regulation, the California Consumer Privacy Act and other privacy statutes. You can find more information on the CCPA in BCLP's California Consumer Privacy Act Practical Guide, and more information about the GDPR in the American Bar Association's The EU GDPR: Answers to the Most Frequently Asked Questions.

Note

    1. California Data Breach Report 2012–2015 (Feb. 2016), http://src.bna.com/cFY.

---

3. THE "FEAR DISPELLER"

Template Structure

Title: *Stop the Fearmongering!:* <<INSERT MISSTATEMENT OR MISUNDERSTANDING>>

Anytime a new statute or regulation comes along, some law firms flag issues that may not be of true concern to companies, or highlight problems that may not, in fact, exist. Unfortunately, that continues to happen in connection with the <<INSERT STATUTE>> where law firms have stated: <<INSERT>>

This is simply incorrect and has caused many companies to unnecessarily be concerned about <<INSERT>>

The following are five examples of (mis)statements that have been made about <<INSERT>>

1. Myth: <<INSERT>>

<<DISCUSS MYTH>>

<<INSERT FACT>>

2. Myth: <<INSERT>>

<<DISCUSS MYTH>>

<<INSERT FACT>>

3. Myth: <<INSERT>>

<<DISCUSS MYTH>>

<<INSERT FACT>>

4. Myth: <<INSERT>>

<<DISCUSS MYTH>>

<<INSERT FACT>>

5. Myth: <<INSERT>>

<<DISCUSS MYTH>>

<<INSERT FACT>>

Example of Its Application

Stop the CCPA Fearmongering: Retailer Loyalty Programs Will Survive

Anytime a new statute or regulation comes along, some law firms unfortunately flag issues that may not be of true concern to companies, or highlight problems that may not, in fact, exist. Unfortunately, that continues to happen in connection with the California Consumer Privacy Act ("CCPA"). In the context of retailer loyalty or reward programs, firms have said that the CCPA may spell the "end of loyalty programs," or implied that the CCPA could lead to "the potential elimination of loyalty programs due to the nondiscrimination requirements." Some law firms have gone so far as to advise retailers to "address the issue[s]" caused by their loyalty programs by "not offer[ing] preferential pricing through loyalty programs" or by "mak[ing] loyalty program pricing available to all customers" regardless of whether they are, in fact, members of the loyalty program. Such changes would, of course, destroy the business-case for having a loyalty program in the first place.

These concerns are incorrect and demonstrate a lack of understanding of the requirements of the CCPA. While the Act is, without a doubt, flawed, poorly drafted, and prone to misinterpretation, it does not lead to the conclusion that most loyalty programs are inherently problematic; nor should it cause most retailers to drastically change the terms and structure of their program. The hyperbolic treatment of loyalty programs by some law firms may also have contributed to several companies and industry groups echoing these concerns with the California legislature and the California Attorney General and alleging (incorrectly) that "the CCPA may prevent[] marketers from offering loyalty programs," or that the CCPA as currently written prohibits "tiered pricing, discounts or coupons."

The following dispels five (mis)statements that have been made in connection with the CCPA's impact on loyalty programs.

1. **Myth: The CCPA prohibits "charging different prices or rates for goods or services."**
   It does not.
   The prohibition against price discrimination in the CCPA only applies to situations in which a consumer exercises a right conferred by the CCPA. Nothing within the CCPA confers a right to join (or not join) a loyalty program. For more information, see FAQ: Is a business prohibited from giving discounts to loyalty program members?

---

continued

2. **Myth: The CCPA states that the benefit provided to the consumer through a loyalty program must be reasonably related to the value provided to the business by the consumer's data.**
It does not.

As indicated above, the CCPA prohibits a business from engaging in price discrimination *when a consumer exercises* a right under the CCPA. The CCPA provides an exception to that prohibition when the discrimination relates to a "price or difference" that is related to the value provided to a business by the consumer's data.

While some lawyers have misinterpreted this as requiring that all loyalty program benefits be related to the value provided to the business by the consumer's data, as noted above, the operation of the loyalty program itself is not prohibited by the CCPA and, thus, does not require the benefit of this exception.

For more information, see FAQ: Does a loyalty program benefit have to relate to the value provided to a business by consumer data?

3. **Myth: Businesses must honor deletion requests for loyalty members.**
They generally do not.

One of the rights conferred by the CCPA is the ability of a consumer to request that a business delete personal information "which the business has collected *from* the consumer." While numerous retailers have expressed confusion regarding whether that right requires the deletion of loyalty program related data, it is important to remember the right to deletion is not an absolute right and may rarely apply in the context of a loyalty program.

As an initial matter, because the right to deletion is limited to information that the business has collected "from" the consumer, if a business receives a deletion request under the CCPA, there is a strong argument that the business is permitted to keep information about the consumer that it developed itself (e.g., its transactions or experiences with the consumer), or information that it received from third parties (e.g., third party businesses that may participate in the loyalty program). As this information was not collected "from" the consumer, it arguably does not fall within the ambit of a deletion right.

In connection with information that is collected directly from a consumer (e.g., name, email address, enrollment details, etc.), there are several exceptions to the CCPA which would allow a business to refuse a deletion request. For more information about each of those exceptions, and a description of how they apply to most loyalty programs, see *FAQ: Is a business required to delete loyalty program information if it receives a deletion request from an active member?* and *FAQ: Is a business required to delete loyalty program information if it receives a deletion request from an inactive member?*

4. Myth: Businesses that offer loyalty programs must include a "do not sell my personal information" link.

Not necessarily.

The CCPA requires that a business that sells personal information disclose within its privacy policy a "list of the categories of personal information it has sold about consumers in the preceding 12 months." The business must then include a link on its homepage titled "Do Not Sell My Personal Information" and allow consumers to opt-out of the sale.

The net result is that if a business sells loyalty program information, the business must disclose that fact and then include a "Do Not Sell" link; if a business does not sell loyalty program information, the business is not required to include such a link.

For more information go to *FAQ: Is a business required to post a "do not sell" link if it offers a loyalty program?*

5. Myth: Businesses that allow consumers to redeem points with third parties are selling information.

They generally are not.

The CCPA broadly defines the term "sale" as including the act of "disclosing" or "making available" personal information "for monetary or other valuable consideration" from one business to another. In the context of loyalty programs, it is not unusual for the operator of a loyalty program to enter into an agreement with a business partner (e.g., another company) to permit a consumer to redeem points accumulated through the loyalty program of business A in order to receive goods or services provided by business B. For example, a hotel may have an agreement with a car rental service through which a consumer can redeem hotel loyalty points to receive a free car rental.

Such redemption arrangements may require the disclosure of personal information from one business (e.g., business A) to a second business (e.g., business B), and may include the payment of money or other consideration for the ability to receive advertising or promotion as a rewards provider. As a result, and depending upon the structure of the business relationships, it is possible that, at first glance, the arrangement could fit the definition of "sale" under the CCPA.

Assuming that the transfer of information to a redemption partner did satisfy the definition of a "sale," the CCPA contains an exception for situations in which a "consumer uses or directs the business to intentionally disclose personal information." As a result, if a consumer uses a loyalty program in order to interact with another business, or directs a loyalty program to disclose personal information as part of a points redemption, the loyalty program operator arguably has not "sold" information.

For more information, go to *FAQ: If a business allows consumers to redeem loyalty program benefits for products or services offered by a partner, does that constitute the sale of information?*

4. THE "FIVE-STEP PROGRAM"; THE "TEN-STEP PROGRAM"

Template Structure

Title: *Five Steps for Avoiding* <<INSERT RISK ISSUE>>

Class action filings concerning <<INSERT>> are rampant with hundreds of new cases filed each month. As damage awards rise, and nuisance settlement values follow suit, companies struggle with how to mitigate risk. As part of a risk-mitigation strategy consider taking the following steps.

1. <<INSERT ACTION 1>>

<<INSERT DESCRIPTION OF ACTION>>

<<INSERT DESCRIPTION OF HOW ACTION MITIGATES RISK>>

2. <<INSERT ACTION 2>>

<<INSERT DESCRIPTION OF ACTION>>

<<INSERT DESCRIPTION OF HOW ACTION MITIGATES RISK>>

3. <<INSERT ACTION 3>>

<<INSERT DESCRIPTION OF ACTION>>

<<INSERT DESCRIPTION OF HOW ACTION MITIGATES RISK>>

4. <<INSERT ACTION 4>>

<<INSERT DESCRIPTION OF ACTION>>

<<INSERT DESCRIPTION OF HOW ACTION MITIGATES RISK>>

5. <<INSERT ACTION 5>>

<<INSERT DESCRIPTION OF ACTION>>

<<INSERT DESCRIPTION OF HOW ACTION MITIGATES RISK>>

Example of Its Application

---

10 Steps to Avoid Wire Transfer Fraud

Businesses are increasingly falling victim to wire fraud scams—sometimes referred to as "man-in-the-email" or "business email compromise" scams. Although there are multiple variants, a common situation involves an attacker gaining access to the email system of a company, or the company's vendor, and monitoring email traffic about an upcoming transaction. When it comes time to submit an invoice or a payment, the attacker impersonates one of the parties and sends wire instructions asking that payment be sent to the attacker's bank account.

Wire fraud scams often victimize two businesses—the business that expected to receive payment, and the business that thought they had made payment. The scam can cause significant contractual disputes between the victims as to who should bear the loss.

Steps to help avoid wire fraud scams:

1. Avoid using free web-based email systems to transact business.
2. Enable multi-factor authentication to log into all email systems.
3. Require employees to select unique and strong passwords or passphrases.
4. Require employees to change email passwords frequently.
5. Require multi-factor authentication (e.g., email and telephone call) when receiving initial payment information.
6. Require multi-factor authentication when receiving a request to change payment information.
7. Send a confirmatory letter or email (not using the "reply" feature in email) concerning any request to change payment information.
8. Delay payment in connection with any request to change payment accounts or a request to make payment to a foreign bank account.
9. Review any request received by email to change payment accounts for signs that the email may be from a third party.
10. Provide clear instructions to business partners concerning how payment information should be communicated.

If you are victimized by wire fraud, consider:

1. Notifying the receiving bank and request that a freeze be placed on any remaining funds.
2. Notifying law enforcement.
3. Investigating whether your email system may have been compromised.
4. Asking business partners to investigate whether their email systems may have been compromised.

5. THE "TRACKER"

Template Structure

Title: <<INSERT REGULATORY ISSUE>> *Tracker*

<<INSERT PARAGRAPH DESCRIBING ISSUE>>

<<INSERT PROCESS FOR FILING REGULATORY PETITION>>

<<INSERT TOTAL PETITIONS PENDING>>

- <<INSERT SUBGROUP OF FILINGS>>
- <<INSERT SUBGROUP OF FILINGS>>

Example of Its Application

November 2019 CCPA Tracker

The California Consumer Privacy Act is considered the most comprehensive federal, or state, privacy statute within the United States. Owing to its hasty drafting (the statute was drafted over a period of seven days), and piecemeal amendments (to-date the statute has been amended seven times) companies, industry groups, and privacy advocates have each sought interpretative guidance from the California Attorney General. We have prepared the following comprehensive summary of pending petitions relating to the scope of the CCPA:

- <<12>> petitions pending.
  - o <<1>> petition to narrow the scope of the CCPA to exclude pharmaceutical companies.
  - o <<2>> petitions to narrow the scope of the CCPA to exclude behavioral advertisers.
  - o <<5>> petitions to expand the scope of the CCPA to include adtech companies.
  - o <<2>> petitions seeking enforcement actions.
  - o <<2>> petitions seeking safe harbor interpretations.

---

6. THE "INDUSTRY BENCHMARK"

Template Structure

Title: *Percentage of* <<INSERT>> <<INCREASED/ DECREASED>>

<<INSERT PARAGRAPH DESCRIBING ISSUE>>

<<INSERT DESCRIPTION OF STUDY OR SURVEY>>

<<INSERT UPDATED RESULTS >>

Example of Its Application (provisions that could easily be swapped in/out by month bracketed)

Websites Deploying a Cookie Banner Increase 15%

The terms "cookie notice" or "cookie banner" refer to a banner, splash page, or other notice that deploys on a website to inform visitors that the site uses cookies. While such disclosures are fairly ubiquitous in the European Union owing to both the General Data Protection Regulation ("GDPR") and the ePrivacy Directive, historically they have been less common in the United States. As companies consider strategies for complying with the CCPA's notice, sharing, service provider, and sale provisions, attention is focusing on whether businesses in the United States will begin to use cookie notices as a compliance or risk mitigation tool.

In order to help companies understand and benchmark industry practice, we analyzed a random sample of the homepages of the Fortune 500 to better understand their use of cookie notices and cookie banners.[1] As of <<INSERT DATE>>, 28% of the Fortune 500's websites were deploying some form of cookie notice.[2] That represents a 15% increase from the previous month.

Notes

1. Using a computer random number generator, BCLP selected 10% of the companies listed among the Fortune 500 in 2019. Revenues for the selected companies ranged from $85 billion to $5 billion. While we did not conduct statistical analysis to determine whether the sample selected accurately represented the range of businesses in the United States, the sample contained companies focused on retail, financials, food, agriculture, manufacturing, entertainment, and energy.

2. Note that some companies in the survey population maintain multiple homepages. For example, a corporation might own several different retail brands each of which maintains its own homepage. The survey focused only on the homepage of the corporate parent (if available) and did not analyze brand-specific practices. If no corporate homepage was available the survey reviewed the website of the company's most prevalent brand.

APPENDIX C

Sample Publication Calendars

JANUARY

Monday	Tuesday	Wednesday	Thursday	Friday	Saturday	Sunday
Monthly Prewritten Article Slot Article Title:	Article Title:	Article Title:	Article Title:	Article Title:	Article Title:	Article Title:
Second Possible Extra Article Slot Article Title:	Article Title:	Article Title:	Article Title:	Article Title:	Article Title:	Article Title:
First Possible Extra Article Slot Article Title:	Article Title:	Article Title:	Article Title:	Article Title:	Article Title:	Article Title:
Article Title:	Article Title:	Article Title:	Article Title:	Article Title:	Article Title:	Article Title:
Article Title:	Article Title:	Article Title:	Article Title:	Article Title:	Article Title:	Article Title:
Article Title:	Article Title:					

FEBRUARY

Monday	Tuesday	Wednesday	Thursday	Friday	Saturday	Sunday
Monthly Prewritten Article Slot Article Title:	Article Title:	Article Title:	Article Title:	Article Title:	Article Title:	Article Title:
Second Possible Extra Article Slot Article Title:	Article Title:	Article Title:	Article Title:	Article Title:	Article Title:	Article Title:
First Possible Extra Article Slot Article Title:	Article Title:	Article Title:	Article Title:	Article Title:	Article Title:	Article Title:
Article Title:	Article Title:	Article Title:	Article Title:	Article Title:	Article Title:	Article Title:
Article Title:	Article Title:	Article Title:	Article Title:	Article Title:	Article Title:	Article Title:
Article Title:	Article Title:					

MARCH

Monday	Tuesday	Wednesday	Thursday	Friday	Saturday	Sunday
Monthly Prewritten Article Slot Article Title:	Article Title:	Article Title:	Article Title:	Article Title:	Article Title:	Article Title:
Second Possible Extra Article Slot Article Title:	Article Title:	Article Title:	Article Title:	Article Title:	Article Title:	Article Title:
First Possible Extra Article Slot Article Title:	Article Title:	Article Title:	Article Title:	Article Title:	Article Title:	Article Title:
Article Title:	Article Title:	Article Title:	Article Title:	Article Title:	Article Title:	Article Title:
Article Title:	Article Title:	Article Title:	Article Title:	Article Title:	Article Title:	Article Title:
Article Title:	Article Title:					

APRIL

Monday	Tuesday	Wednesday	Thursday	Friday	Saturday	Sunday
Monthly Prewritten Article Slot Article Title:	Article Title:	Article Title:	Article Title:	Article Title:	Article Title:	Article Title:
Second Possible Extra Article Slot Article Title:	Article Title:	Article Title:	Article Title:	Article Title:	Article Title:	Article Title:
First Possible Extra Article Slot Article Title:	Article Title:	Article Title:	Article Title:	Article Title:	Article Title:	Article Title:
Article Title:	Article Title:	Article Title:	Article Title:	Article Title:	Article Title:	Article Title:
Article Title:	Article Title:	Article Title:	Article Title:	Article Title:	Article Title:	Article Title:
Article Title:	Article Title:					

MAY

Monday	Tuesday	Wednesday	Thursday	Friday	Saturday	Sunday
Monthly Prewritten Article Slot Article Title:	Article Title:	Article Title:	Article Title:	Article Title:	Article Title:	Article Title:
Second Possible Extra Article Slot Article Title:	Article Title:	Article Title:	Article Title:	Article Title:	Article Title:	Article Title:
First Possible Extra Article Slot Article Title:	Article Title:	Article Title:	Article Title:	Article Title:	Article Title:	Article Title:
Article Title:	Article Title:	Article Title:	Article Title:	Article Title:	Article Title:	Article Title:
Article Title:	Article Title:	Article Title:	Article Title:	Article Title:	Article Title:	Article Title:
Article Title:	Article Title:					

JUNE

Monday	Tuesday	Wednesday	Thursday	Friday	Saturday	Sunday
Monthly Prewritten Article Slot Article Title:	Article Title:	Article Title:	Article Title:	Article Title:	Article Title:	Article Title:
Second Possible Extra Article Slot Article Title:	Article Title:	Article Title:	Article Title:	Article Title:	Article Title:	Article Title:
First Possible Extra Article Slot Article Title:	Article Title:	Article Title:	Article Title:	Article Title:	Article Title:	Article Title:
Article Title:	Article Title:	Article Title:	Article Title:	Article Title:	Article Title:	Article Title:
Article Title:	Article Title:	Article Title:	Article Title:	Article Title:	Article Title:	Article Title:
Article Title:	Article Title:					

JULY

Monday	Tuesday	Wednesday	Thursday	Friday	Saturday	Sunday
Monthly Prewritten Article Slot Article Title:	Article Title:	Article Title:	Article Title:	Article Title:	Article Title:	Article Title:
Second Possible Extra Article Slot Article Title:	Article Title:	Article Title:	Article Title:	Article Title:	Article Title:	Article Title:
First Possible Extra Article Slot Article Title:	Article Title:	Article Title:	Article Title:	Article Title:	Article Title:	Article Title:
Article Title:	Article Title:	Article Title:	Article Title:	Article Title:	Article Title:	Article Title:
Article Title:	Article Title:	Article Title:	Article Title:	Article Title:	Article Title:	Article Title:
Article Title:	Article Title:					

AUGUST

Monday	Tuesday	Wednesday	Thursday	Friday	Saturday	Sunday
Monthly Prewritten Article Slot Article Title:	Article Title:	Article Title:	Article Title:	Article Title:	Article Title:	Article Title:
Second Possible Extra Article Slot Article Title:	Article Title:	Article Title:	Article Title:	Article Title:	Article Title:	Article Title:
First Possible Extra Article Slot Article Title:	Article Title:	Article Title:	Article Title:	Article Title:	Article Title:	Article Title:
Article Title:	Article Title:	Article Title:	Article Title:	Article Title:	Article Title:	Article Title:
Article Title:	Article Title:	Article Title:	Article Title:	Article Title:	Article Title:	Article Title:
Article Title:	Article Title:					

SEPTEMBER

Monday	Tuesday	Wednesday	Thursday	Friday	Saturday	Sunday
Monthly Prewritten Article Slot Article Title:	Article Title:	Article Title:	Article Title:	Article Title:	Article Title:	Article Title:
Second Possible Extra Article Slot Article Title:	Article Title:	Article Title:	Article Title:	Article Title:	Article Title:	Article Title:
First Possible Extra Article Slot Article Title:	Article Title:	Article Title:	Article Title:	Article Title:	Article Title:	Article Title:
Article Title:	Article Title:	Article Title:	Article Title:	Article Title:	Article Title:	Article Title:
Article Title:	Article Title:	Article Title:	Article Title:	Article Title:	Article Title:	Article Title:
Article Title:	Article Title:					

OCTOBER

Monday	Tuesday	Wednesday	Thursday	Friday	Saturday	Sunday
Monthly Prewritten Article Slot Article Title:	Article Title:	Article Title:	Article Title:	Article Title:	Article Title:	Article Title:
Second Possible Extra Article Slot Article Title:	Article Title:	Article Title:	Article Title:	Article Title:	Article Title:	Article Title:
First Possible Extra Article Slot Article Title:	Article Title:	Article Title:	Article Title:	Article Title:	Article Title:	Article Title:
Article Title:	Article Title:	Article Title:	Article Title:	Article Title:	Article Title:	Article Title:
Article Title:	Article Title:	Article Title:	Article Title:	Article Title:	Article Title:	Article Title:
Article Title:	Article Title:					

NOVEMBER

Monday	Tuesday	Wednesday	Thursday	Friday	Saturday	Sunday
Monthly Prewritten Article Slot Article Title:	Article Title:	Article Title:	Article Title:	Article Title:	Article Title:	Article Title:
Second Possible Extra Article Slot Article Title:	Article Title:	Article Title:	Article Title:	Article Title:	Article Title:	Article Title:
First Possible Extra Article Slot Article Title:	Article Title:	Article Title:	Article Title:	Article Title:	Article Title:	Article Title:
Article Title:	Article Title:	Article Title:	Article Title:	Article Title:	Article Title:	Article Title:
Article Title:	Article Title:	Article Title:	Article Title:	Article Title:	Article Title:	Article Title:
Article Title:	Article Title:					

DECEMBER

Monday	Tuesday	Wednesday	Thursday	Friday	Saturday	Sunday
Monthly Prewritten Article Slot Article Title:	Article Title:	Article Title:	Article Title:	Article Title:	Article Title:	Article Title:
Second Possible Extra Article Slot Article Title:	Article Title:	Article Title:	Article Title:	Article Title:	Article Title:	Article Title:
First Possible Extra Article Slot Article Title:	Article Title:	Article Title:	Article Title:	Article Title:	Article Title:	Article Title:
Article Title:	Article Title:	Article Title:	Article Title:	Article Title:	Article Title:	Article Title:
Article Title:	Article Title:	Article Title:	Article Title:	Article Title:	Article Title:	Article Title:
Article Title:	Article Title:					

APPENDIX D

Sheet for Article Self-Analysis

Rule	Present	Comments
Rule 1: Efficient Writing	☐	
Rule 2: Short	☐	
Rule 3: Business Practical	☐	
Rule 4: Shelf Stable	☐	
Rule 5: Recycling and the Rule of Threes	☐	
Rule 6: Metrics	☐	
Rule 7: Repetition and Stockpiling	☐	
Rule 8: Do It Yourself	☐